Praise for
The DNA of D6

The DNA of D6 is a powerful and practical family ministry book that I wholeheartedly recommend to every pastor, ministry leader, and parent who cares about healthy churches and Christ-centered families.

Timothy Paul Jones, Ph.D.
Professor of Christian Family Ministry,
Southern Baptist Theological Seminary
Author of *Perspectives on Family Ministry* and
The Family Ministry Field Guide

Ron Hunter and D6 are at the center of an amazing shift in family ministry in the Church. *The DNA of D6* movement is a solid strategy of doing generational discipleship right.

Jim Burns, Ph.D.
President, HomeWord
Author of *Confident Parenting, Getting Ready for Marriage,* and *Pass It On*

Finally! This book is long overdue. It's simply the best family ministry and generational discipleship book ever.

Les Parrott, Ph.D.
Author of *Saving Your Marriage Before It Starts*

If you're really serious about disciplining kids and families, then *The DNA of D6* is your starting point.

Dale Hudson
Director of Children's Ministries, Christ Fellowship Church
Writer at www.relevantchildrensministry.com

D6 ministry's hardwiring is "not about the next generation—it is about every generation."

Dr. Steve Vandegriff
Professor, Department of Christian Leadership
and Church Ministries
at Liberty University

If you want to be a D6 church, you'll want to get this strategy manual.

Dr. Scott Turansky
National Center for Biblical Parenting

Ron Hunter offers us wisdom and advice, which youth workers and the entire church staff should read, consider, and enlist.

Dr. Walt Mueller
Center for Parent/Youth Understanding

The DNA of D6 is one of the best books I've read on discipleship. I have required it for several of our staff to read!

Chris Truett
Senior Pastor, Bethel FWB Church
Kinston, NC

Ron Hunter offers a series of dynamic questions, conversations, and essential Scriptures, which God can use to accelerate your church's impact for generations to come.

Rob Rienow
Founder of Visionary Family Ministries
VisionaryFam.com

This concise resource can begin credible and productive discussions and plans for families and ministry leaders.

Tommy Sanders, Ph.D.
Vice President of Academic and Graduate Programs and professor of religion at East Texas Baptist University

The DNA of D6 is a timely and critical resource for the church today. Ron provides both hope and a roadmap to help the church partner with parents to accomplish their most important task—discipling their kids. This book is easy to read, and is full of memorable and practical steps for passing on the faith to the next generation.

Sean McDowell, Ph.D.
Professor at Biola University, international speaker, and best-selling author of over 15 books (seanmcdowell.org)

Ron Hunter has stimulated our thinking towards a refocus on generational discipleship.

Christopher Talbot
Program Coordinator for Youth & Family Ministry
Welch College

Ron Hunter has written a primer for generational discipleship that connects the church and home for maximum impact. He has brilliantly set the local church up for unique and effective strategic implementation, as it should be.

Brian Haynes
Lead Pastor, Bay Area First Baptist Church
Author of *Shift* and *The Legacy Path*

My good friend Ron Hunter has outdone himself with his book, *The DNA of D6*. We have enriched our focus on families by using many of the things we have gleaned and then discussed as a staff. Ron is one of the most gifted leaders I know and this book is a must have for every ministry leader's book shelf.

Chad Overton
Minister to Children
Houston's First Baptist Church, Texas

This book vividly illustrates the power of parental influence and generational discipleship in raising children to be followers of Jesus.

Jason Caillier
Professor and Director of Master of Arts in Family Ministry
Dallas Baptist University

If you're brand new to the D6 message or a seasoned veteran, this book will guide you in the process of developing a solid family ministry that reaches and excites the homes in your church and community.

Ted Cunningham
Founding Pastor, Woodland Hills Family Church
Author of *The Power of Home* and *Fun Loving You*

In *The DNA of D6*, Ron Hunter presents a comprehensive guide for how today's congregation can both equip and serve families and parents in a biblical partnership for generational discipleship. In *The DNA of D6*, Ron's heart for strengthening the family is evident, and his love for the church shines through.

Chap Clark, Ph.D.
Editor and contributor, *21st Century Youth Ministry – Five Views*
Professor of Youth, Family, and Culture
Fuller Theological Seminary

In *The DNA of D6*, Ron Hunter clearly lays out a plan for linking church and home in that valuable process of generational discipleship. Church leaders need to absorb every word.

Richard Ross, Ph.D.
Professor of youth ministry
Southwestern Seminary
RichardRoss.com

Let Ron and *The DNA of D6* re-impassion you for ministry.

Dannah Gresh
Best-selling author and Founder of Secret Keeper Girl

My friend Ron Hunter is nothing short of a world-class spiritual DNA expert. Ron understands the building blocks God uses to build strong families and strong children. He shares them in a way that's real, really understandable, and really needed by parents today. The D6 Movement that Ron launched has revolutionized faith formation in hundreds of churches across our country. Now, at last, there's a book that YOU can take home and see these incredible D6 principles impact in YOUR LIFE, your faith, and your children's faith today!

John Trent, Ph.D.
Gary D. Chapman Chair of Marriage and Family Ministry
and Therapy at Moody Theological Seminary
Author of *The Blessing* and *LifeMapping*

Ron Hunter has provided a refreshing look at generational discipleship—arguably the most important ministry concept facing the church today. *The DNA of D6* provides the necessary leadership principles that will produce the habits needed for healthier believers and corporate church bodies. The practical nature of this book provides the church leader with concepts that can be adapted to any local church ministry. This is more than a novel idea. It is a foundational catalyst for change, and it begins with you!

Ron Davis
Director of Student Life
Southeastern FWB College

As a Lead Pastor, I am constantly searching for ways to ensure that the families God has chosen to intersect with us are equipped and empowered to lead their homes as best as possible. Through practical instruction, solid dialogue, and encouragement, *The DNA of D6* acts as an incredible resource to allow the local church to act as an extension of the home, not its replacement. Great work.

Mike Butler
Lead Pastor
CrossPointe Church, Norman OK

Finally! A comprehensive guide to practically implementing family ministry into the heart of the church. Ron Hunter absolutely hit a home run with *The DNA of D6!* This book is the perfect resource for the local church looking to help its families move beyond the burdensome, disappointing status quo and embrace God's original intention for them—to make their home a discipleship center to build a legacy of thriving faith.

Tommy Swindol
Discipleship Pastor
The Donelson Fellowship

THE
DNA
D6
of

BUILDING BLOCKS
of Generational Discipleship

RON HUNTER JR.

randall house

Published by Randall House
114 Bush Road
Nashville, TN 37217
www.randallhouse.com

Printed in the United States of America

13- ISBN 9780892656554

To the Randall House team—a family dedicated to "Helping Build Believers through Church and Home" and to our wise and supportive board of directors.

Table of Contents

DEUTERONOMY 6:5-7

YOU SHALL LOVE THE LORD YOUR GOD WITH ALL YOUR HEART AND
WITH ALL YOUR SOUL AND WITH ALL YOUR MIGHT. And these words
that I command you today shall be on your heart. You shall teach them
diligently to your children, and shall talk of them when you sit in your
house, and when you walk by the way, and when you lie down, and
when you rise.

Preface

(From the Author: The leadership team at Randall House approached me in 2014 about writing this book about what God is doing in leading the D6 movement. Part of this journey would not have been possible without my friend, Matt Markins, cofounder of the D6 Conference. For six years, he and I traveled many miles together, shared blue-sky sessions, and engaged with church leaders—and we continue our friendship today. He has since gone to help lead Awana through some strategic changes. I have asked him to share this portion of the story.)

Before coming to Randall House, Ron Hunter pastored for eleven years. During the last three, he caught the vision for family ministry and left the senior pastorate. He moved to a place where he could focus solely on his passion: discipleship and family ministry. Because of his work and philosophy in local church ministry, Ron was hired at a relatively young age to replace the retiring CEO of Randall House.

His position there provided an opportunity to change the antiquated approach to discipleship held by most churches. In 2004, Ron led our Randall House team in a significant change as they worked to develop a curriculum based on the principles taught in Deuteronomy 6, placing emphasis on both church and home. Other publishers and resource providers soon followed. In 2006, he came up with the term "D6." We spotlighted the message of Deuteronomy 6 in a way that connected with church leaders, volunteers, and parents, inspiring these audiences to a greater level of community.

In February of 2007, Ron hosted an offsite retreat for select team leaders. He invited five ministry leaders (lead pastors and youth pastors from different regions of the United States) to review and critique the effectiveness of the ministry of Randall House. This was a critical gathering as we were trying to understand some of the greatest challenges facing the church and families. And at this gathering, the initial inspiration for the D6 Conference surfaced.

If we were going to be effective in coming alongside churches in the area of disciple making, we could not do it alone. Ron and I began to dream about developing an environment where ministry leaders and parents could gather as a like-minded community to advance the cause of disciple making and family ministry. (Ron later termed this *generational discipleship*). We envisioned this gathering to be a place where a commitment to the gospel, Scripture, and disciple making was central, but the methodological ideas could vary. An open-source platform in family ministry did not exist at that time. The goal was a generation of young people who would catapult right out of high school or college into a life of Christ-centered mission and worship. We knew this would require that these young people be surrounded by a church and family engaged in their faith formation and discipleship journey.

In the summer of 2008, we launched our marketing plan fourteen months before the first conference. As we engaged with church leaders from all over the nation, a common response was, "We've prayed for a conference and community like this! I'll be there with my entire team!"

Ron and I prayed for specific items and details that had to come together. God answered each request. When criticism came and challenges arose, we were able to move forward with obedience and a deep confidence from the Holy Spirit because this was not our conference. It was not our movement. It was not our audience. It was His. We were simply God's servants and stewards of His message: "The Lord our God is one . . . love Him . . . impress His Word on your children."

Matt Markins
Awana
Vice President of Ministry Resources
Vice President of Marketing and Strategy

1 Where to Begin?

God is the architect of the brilliant plan to capture the hearts of the generations.[1] —Brian Haynes

When you walk into Starbucks, does the barista start making your favorite drink even before you order? Mine is a venti seven-pump (don't judge me) white chocolate mocha. What about your favorite ice cream flavor? Not only do I have a favorite flavor, but I have a favorite brand: Ben and Jerry's "Chunky Monkey."

It's uncanny how our brand loyalty keeps us coming back. Let's try some brand trivia and see if you can name the companies associated with the following slogans:

- "Think different"
- "The ultimate driving machine"
- "Never stop improving"
- "More saving. More doing."
- "Be your own beautiful"
- "They're grrrrreat"
- "Building believers through church and home"

In order, the answers are Apple, BMW, Lowe's, Home Depot, Vera Bradley, and Kellogg's Frosted Flakes. And that last slogan? Well, it is ours—D6.

Each of these cultural brands discovered how to meet the needs of people in uniquely different ways. Some products have changed our culture and the way we live our lives. Remember when people could argue the facts or try to remember who starred in a certain movie? Today, instead of friendly discussions, we whip out our phones and Google—discussion over, new culture. Google made their brand into the cultural lexicon. These new cultural norms did not happen overnight, but they have completely changed our values and routines.

D6, a curriculum since 2004—a movement since 2009, is about *generational discipleship*, the new cultural term for churches who care deeply about every age and who use family ministry to accomplish new norms for their church. Shifting values and routines is not easy, but when churches see the benefits, the result is similar to paying for that amazing five-dollar cup of coffee.

The DNA of D6 will walk you through what it takes to build a new culture that loves and values every age. Even in traditional churches, a congregation can readily adopt new and more beneficial habits. The result will be healthy children, teens, adults, and senior adults. We cannot medically change our DNA, but we can alter habits to become healthier. And churches *can* change their DNA when ministry leaders equip people for ministry rather than just do ministry.

How to Use This Book

The DNA of D6 provides any church with the stimulus to plan, strategize, evaluate, and refine its discipleship and more specifically its family ministry. While it is comprehensive for ministry leaders laying the foundation for an intentional generational discipleship ministry, it is also helpful for those who are further into this arena and just need some refinement. It does not matter if you have no staff, a small staff, or a large staff. The principle of this book is about the church helping the home, and any size church can do this.

This book also carries a warning: Do not read it alone. Instead, find another staff member or volunteer to read along with you so you can bounce ideas and implementation strategies as you go. Work through the chapter-ending questions and compare your responses. Better yet, give copies of this book to your staff and/or volunteer team and meet regularly to work through the chapters together.

So—where to begin? When you open the map application on your phone, you see a blue dot representing where you are now. Once you have determined your destination, a red digital pushpin represents the goal. Download the free *DNA of D6 Generational Discipleship Assessment* to help you and your leaders determine where you are right now. After self-scoring your results, you will have identified areas for improvement that correspond to various chapters found in this book. Consider having all of your small group leaders, staff, and lead volunteers take it with you. You can find it at d6family.com/dna.

As you read, you, too, must decide what is right for your church. Never confuse program implementation with the principles to implement—the first can be almost anything, and the second never changes. In the Great Commission, the principle to implement requires sharing the gospel. But the program implementation may take many forms, such as one-on-one conversations or social media. This book will walk you through more principles and lead you just close enough to implementation or practices to discover what is best for your situation without disregarding the principles.

At the end of every chapter, you'll find a section called "D6 Connection." Here, we offer both questions to consider and resources to check out. Both will help you personalize the chapter content to your specific church and ministry situation. Just as you need the families in your church to move beyond merely reading the Bible or hearing it taught in church to studying it and applying it to their lives, you will need to go beyond a simple reading of this book. In order to build or evaluate your generational discipleship strategy, do not rush through the chapters, but read with care and make sure to take time for the D6 Connection. Once you've finished the questions, compare answers with the volunteers and/or staff members who are walking through the book alongside you.

D6 is here to help, so let's agree to work together in an endeavor ordained by God to change not only individual lives but generations yet to come.

The Definition of Family

The context of Scripture is clear: God defines *family* as generations of dads and moms influencing their children and grandchildren. He designed and talked about the ideal home as having a dad and mom loving one or more children in the way He, our heavenly Father, loves us. He intends parents to coach their kids toward spiritual growth so they in turn will do the same for their kids.

We must recognize we do not live in an ideal society. It was never God's desire for marriages to end in divorce, and yet throughout Scripture, He used and blessed single moms. The family is not always an ideal set of parents and kids all doing what God intended. The Bible reminds of adapted models of generational discipleship. The often quoted and normal succession of teaching flows from father to son and on to grandson as seen in Abraham, Isaac, and Jacob. There is not always a godly father or mother as evidenced in Mordecai teaching his niece Esther. Or how (Titus 1:4) Paul mentored his adopted son in the faith, Titus. Notice how Timothy's faithful mother seemed to carry the whole spiritual lead of parental influence. Regardless of what season of life, God can use you to teach someone in your family or someone adopted by way of friendships and connections.

Traditional: Abraham, Isaac, Jacob

Related: Mordecai, Esther

One Parent: Eunice, Timothy

Adopted: Paul, Titus

By default and for a myriad of reasons, grandparents sometimes raise their grandchildren. The vital truth to remember is God wants the church to help shape the home—even if broken or damaged—into what He intends. When this book refers to coaching "parents," the term may suggest a dad and mom, stepparents, a single dad, a single mom, adoptive parents, or grandparents.

Build or Move?

I want to share a conversation I've had numerous times with those seeking a ministry position. It goes something like this:

"Hey Ron, do you know of a church that is serious about D6 and looking for a family minister?"

"If they're serious about D6, don't you think they already have a family minister?"

They push a little harder. "My church does not understand Deuteronomy 6, and I'm passionate about working in such an environment."

"Well, do you consider yourself a leader or a manager?"

"A leader, why?" they shoot back.

"A leader goes in and changes the culture over time, but a manager just oversees what others have already changed," I explain. "Maybe God is calling you to help people discover D6 and make the changes even if it takes a bit of patience and effort."

Churches are rediscovering the revitalizing affect of implementing a D6 philosophy. While the number of D6-oriented churches is small compared to the whole population of churches, this community is rapidly growing. These churches have implemented a long-term generational discipleship strategy. Leaders help followers discover why and how by walking them through the cultural change model to take the church to a D6 culture.

Will you lead or manage? Your answer will determine if you wish to move to a church already doing D6 or take the bold step of helping establish a D6 culture in more churches.

Urgency

The tribe who cooks over fire and remains unaware of stoves sees no need to change. Ground beef tastes pretty good until you eat a rib eye. A needle and thimble does the job until you realize a sewing machine can do so much more in a shorter time.

Compare the ones who know to the ones who do not, and the sense of urgency is as far apart as the experiences. True leaders understand that their followers often feel less urgency than they do. The church, like the classic frog in the kettle, often fails to realize how terminal its environment has become.

The Pace of Change

Think back to when you were small and played on the merry-go-round. Do you remember pushing as fast as you could and then hopping on? How fast would it turn?

Let's say you and your best friend try pushing together. You both jump on, but you move to the middle, and your friend stays on the outside as it spins. Which one of you is traveling the fastest?

Although the merry-go-round travels at the same number of revolutions per minute, your friend is traveling faster. That's because the distance he or she must travel is greater than the distance you must travel to reach the same spot at the same time. Just think of this as sprocket science.

Or think about a NASCAR race. When two cars round the entire curve side by side, the one on the outside is going faster because it covers more distance. And just as it is scarier to be the outside car trying to keep up and on the line, your church members will always feel like they are catching up and traveling faster just to reach the place where you have already traveled in less time. For ministry leaders, it is never fast enough; for church members, well, they might need a barf bag.

Use wisdom when affecting change. Never confuse a "yes" vote in a business or leadership council meeting with everyone buying in and working toward the goal. The United States outlawed unfair treatment of African-Americans through several pieces of legislation prior to Martin Luther King, Jr.'s hard work to get people on both sides to think differently about racism. How many times have you gotten the church to vote "yes," but then no attendance or financial support follows?

Spend time with decision-makers and influencers and hold multiple conversations. Cultural change by its nature takes more time than expected. The church has ignored D6 principles for several generations, and moving back to generational discipleship will take longer than a year or two.

How long? Each church is different. It may take a year to realize the need. Each year after may bring the congregation one step closer to a cultural change that results in a healthy D6 church. Remember, it is not about the next generation—it is about *every* generation. When you understand that statement, generational discipleship is non-negotiable.

When you and your team finish this book, you'll share a vision for developing generational gladiators who will fight for the development of the next generation. The younger one will aspire to be a part of the next older group, and you will have closed the gaps through which people depart from church and from the faith. It's time to revitalize by building believers through church and home. This is a D6 church.

D6 Connection

Questions

The church can begin to grasp the value and advantage to a cultural change by helping its staff and volunteers discover the potential by asking certain questions. These are just the beginning steps to help multiply and share the D6 vision. The goal is to stretch the way people think so new ideas about generational discipleship will surface. Please understand that here in the beginning stage of our journey through this material, the questions are designed more to start discussions than provide definitive answers. Let the D6 discussions begin!

- What are our church families' greatest needs? (Do not focus solely on dysfunctional needs; the church needs to move from ER mindset to preventative care.)
- How can we connect parents to their kids more often?
- How can we connect grandparents to their grandkids either here or some distance?
- What are the most important tools we can give to parents?
- Which kids need to be "spiritually adopted" because their parents are absent?
- How can we connect empty-nest parents to other parents still raising kids or to kids who have uninvolved parents?
- How are the needs of parents different at various stages of parenting?

- How does the health of marriages affect parenting skills?
- Who can you get to come spend time with your leadership team and volunteers to develop a D6 mindset?
- What conference would your whole team benefit from experiencing together?
- What three churches should our staff visit together and interact with their staff?

Resources

Family Ministry Field Guide: How Your Church Can Equip Parents to Make Disciples by Timothy Paul Jones

Partnering with Parents in Youth Ministry: The Practical Guide to Today's Family-Based Youth Ministry by Jim Burns and Mark DeVries

Rethink by Steven Wright

Sticky Faith by Dr. Kara E. Powell and Dr. Chap Clark

Youth Ministry in the 21st Century: Five Views by Chap Clark, Fernando Arzola Jr., Greg Stier, Ron Hunter Jr., and Brian Cosby.

2

1/168:
Flawed Fraction or
Ministry Multiplier

*There is little difference in an unavailable dad
versus an absentee dad.*[1]—Thomas Hoffmaster

"That's a small number!"

"What does that number mean?"

"One hundred sixty-eight what?"

These are some of the responses I hear when I wear a T-shirt sold by our organization. The fraction 1/168 printed on the front is almost guaranteed to elicit questions. It opens the door to some great conversations.

To grasp this tiny number, try cutting a round pie or cake into one hundred sixty-eight equal pieces. This denominator stands for the number of hours in a week. The scary part is what the numerator (one) represents: the average number of hours a student spends in discipleship each week. This figure comes from thirty minutes of teaching received in a life group, small group, or class and another thirty minutes of listening to the senior pastor or youth pastor. The back of the 1/168 T-shirt displays the phrase "It's not enough" and, as a source for answers, the website D6family.com.

If a child receives on average only one hour of spiritual influence per week, how does your church acquire more opportunities to provide coaching or instruction? The primary way is to multiply your ministry by getting parents involved during the family's time at home. It is time to change the numerator and make it a bigger number!

Parent Power

Whether you realize it or not, parents are your greatest ministry multipliers. Look at the amount of influence you and others have on your children. Your first child crawled everywhere. You took pictures, tons of pictures. You recorded every milestone—until your third child came along. Based on his or her baby book, this child barely existed. But the firstborn had your full attention. One day, you observed his or her first step, pulling up beside the couch, then letting go with one hand and turning toward the middle of the room—risking it all and letting go, one step, two steps, and plop, the fall.

Your little one looked up from this crumpled position to see your reaction—what you did, what you said, and how you looked—to *interpret the moment.* If you seemed scared or upset, the crying commenced. If you cheered or clapped, the laughing began. Through the developmental years and into adolescence, your child interpreted the world through your reactions.

Why do my own son and daughter support a college football team back in our home state when we moved away when they were just five and six? They cheer, wear the colors, and watch faithfully because their mom and I do. And their grandmother screams and yells even louder. The kids caught the spirit and became fans because of the influence of family.

From their earliest moments, kids take their cues from their parents. They are later influenced by others, but never to the same degree as by the core values taught by dads and moms. Parents inspire and shape their child's desires and gripes. Into their teen years and beyond, your kids tend to laugh at what you laugh at and fear what you fear. Their root attitudes come from watching how Dad and Mom interpret life. Think about how you view the following items and how similar or opposite these views are to those of your parents: money, politics, authority, education, sports, race, death, and holidays.

The power and legacy of family influence runs deep and touches multiple areas. If parents respect law enforcement and authority figures, the kids will honor positions and titles. Parents determine how a child manages money: whether or not they budget and how they deal with debt or savings. Parents' routines around the holidays determine if gifts are opened on Christmas Eve or Day, if birthdays are a big deal, and if the family must endure the Macy's Thanksgiving Day Parade. If Dad and Mom value education; read to their kids; and do not discount math, science, or history, then the child will probably be a good student with great likelihood to complete undergrad and possibly graduate work. Parents' values prompt attitudes, actions, and accomplishments.

Generational Power

Does this premise hold up biblically? Think about one of the genealogies noted most often in Scripture: Abraham, Isaac, and Jacob. What did the sons learn from the fathers? Although the biblical greats are most known for their roles as the patriarchs of the nation of Israel, they were far from perfect, and each father passed along his character flaws to his son.

Notice the small thread of deception that grew when Abraham lied about Sarah being his wife by claiming her as his sister (Genesis 20). His son Isaac later faced a similar situation (Genesis 26). Like his dad, he lied about Rebekah, his wife, suggesting she was his sister to preserve his own well-being. When Isaac's son was born, the name he received described the person he was: Jacob—heel catcher, supplanter (one taking the place of another), and trickster or deceiver.

This trickster took advantage of his older brother twice. When his brother, Esau, was weak, hungry, and desperate, Jacob conned him out of his birthright by coercing him to trade it for a mess of pottage. But the worst deception was the second one, when he deceived his almost-blind father by pretending to be his brother and stealing Esau's blessing.

Jacob's accomplice? His mom. His model? His dad. Jacob, his dad, and his granddad all lied to get something they wanted—what an inheritance! And we thought we had a lock on dysfunction.

Similarly, womanizing and misplaced priorities were passed from David to Solomon and on to Rehoboam. But notice the ways the passage outlining the Ten Commandments discusses the implications of generations. Read the Exodus 20 narrative and underline the following generational verses: Exodus 20:5-6, 10, and 12. Deuteronomy 5 also reiterates the Ten Commandments. Read with emphasis the following verses: Deuteronomy 5:9-10, 14, 16, and 29. This passage leads into the foundational passage of Deuteronomy 6:5-9, the Shema, the same one dedicated Jews quote each morning. The Shema does not emphasize the rules of the Ten Commandments, but rather what parents should pass along to their kids: how Dad and Mom love God and love His Word enough to make it a part of their daily life. Deuteronomy 6 speaks to parents in the same way Proverbs 1:8 speaks to children. Both emphasize an instructional relationship.

Never underestimate the influence of the previous generation. Genesis 18:19 calls parents to instruct kids and live out a consistent relationship with the Lord. Exodus 12:26-27 and 13:14-15 show how Dad and Mom can point out the presence of God and His power within a family. This helps kids build trust in Him for their future. Seven hundred years later, God says the same thing in Isaiah 38:19. Going forward nearly another eight hundred years, Paul reaches back to the faith of Timothy's grandparents (2 Timothy 1:3-5) when instructing him about the faith-legacy of his ancestors.

Because parents do not naturally assume this role, the church must show them how to do it. Show dads how to tell the story of the way God's intervention, sustaining power, strength, wisdom, or other presence helped at a significant junction. With the right tools, the family's perspective on God's involvement will go beyond major events. Parents bring the reality and influence of God into the home by showing the kids how to follow Him rather than charting just any course on their own. In Chapter 3, you will see some of these same parental models through a slightly different lens. Our task as leaders is to help parents see that our family challenge is not a new one and that God prescribed a solution from the beginning.

Daniel, Shadrach, Meshach, and Abednego cheered for the God of their parents even when living in a foreign land. My kids cheer for our college team, and they also tend to value what my wife and I value—good or bad. College football is not all there is in this world. Parents need to emphasize and cheer for God the way we cheer for our sports teams. Think about it—we dress for our team, we know the players, the stats, the opponents, and we set aside appointed time to spend in this worship (yes, I meant to use that word) each week. Apply this devotion to God, and see how your kids respond.

Eating Up the Denominator

If parents have such a great amount of influence, why does the numerator still show only "1," and what can we do to change it? The logical question is, "If only one hour is spent in discipleship, what is eating up the remaining 168 hours?"

Of course, sleep consumes a big portion of this number. Arguably, most kids do not get eight hours a night, but let us assume they get seven, and that takes forty-nine hours. School absorbs another seven hours a day, taking thirty-five more hours, or five days. So after eighty-four hours for sleep and school, that leaves half the week, or another eighty-four hours—the same ones to which God referred in Deuteronomy 6. That's time spent getting up, commuting, eating, and talking. We often miss these opportune times in the busy-ness of the day or by absorbing some form of media. Let's examine how media captures our time and eats the denominator.

Phones, for example, captivate us in ways they never have before. I cannot imagine living without the convenience of my iPhone. I wonder how pastors did it back in the days before computers. Yes, mobile technology can have some positive spiritual benefits. According to Barna research, one in four adults has increased in time spent reading the Bible due to downloading an app.[2] Mobile devices provide some impressive Bible apps and ways to interact for our quiet time. Technology simplifies our world and provides efficiency, but if you are honest, you will admit it also enslaves you at times. I am referring not only to work-dominated habits, but social ones as well.

And we cannot overlook still another thief of time: television. Each week, your kids watch enough hours of TV to equal the hours of a full-time job, reported a 2013 study. The same study also revealed that the typical child spends an average of thirty-five hours per week watching TV and another ten hours on a gaming system.[3] An older study showed that ninety-nine percent of Americans owned at least one television, and the average amount of time a TV was on in the home is six hours and forty-seven minutes.[4] The passage of time has doubtless increased those figures.

Sixty-six percent of families eat dinner while watching TV, a California State University of Northridge study showed.[5] Other studies reveal a close link between the family dinner table and outcomes in a child's life. The CSUN study also reported *meaningful conversation* between parents and kids each week averaged only three and a half minutes,[6] far worse than the 1/168 number. The parenting number has to grow.

Having worked in the field of marketing and television, I want to remind you how powerful it is to *see* someone peeling a lemon, breaking open the wedges while juice squirts in all directions, and tossing a wedge into their mouth to bite. Is your mouth salivating over the imagined sour flavor? Neither radio nor print brings a response like this, a fact which has sold many commercials. And when you combine visual, audible, and tactile (in mobile devices) senses, the power of influence rises exponentially. Television's and video's messaging and philosophy stimulate kids (and adults) through inspiration, assumed authority, and effect because of power of the medium used.

Ask yourself who gets to shape the worldview of the kids in your church: their parents or the Kardashians? Because of the powerful impact of multiple hours in front of the TV, it truly is hard for parents to keep up.

All this means that whether in the form of tablets, phones, television, gaming systems, or other items, rectangles consume your—and especially your kids'—world. How many times do you see a person or persons standing or sitting in a group, but not a true part of it because of their interaction with some electronic rectangle?

Our fascination with mobile devices has created connected isolation. Half of all millennials admit to allowing their personal electronics to separate them from other people, and thirty-five percent (just over one in three) of all adults admit the same thing. Worse, only twenty-one percent of these hyperlinked adults set aside any time to connect with God.[7] The typical response? "I don't have time." In truth, time is the true equalizer, because everyone has the same 168 hours.

The technology-based rectangles in our lives can provide tremendous value, but should not control us. We need food, but in moderate proportions. In the same way a scale helps us monitor the results of our food choices, perhaps we also need a scale to weigh our electronic usage and keep us within a healthy range. As church leaders, we must make it our mission to help parents change that flawed fraction.

Raising the Numerator

And parents can change it. It is not totally fair to suggest that if the church has one hour, then the parents or home have all of the other 167, but they do have enough hours equivalent to a part-time job and that's their full-time job! Both dads and moms can look for more ways to interact with their kids than just sharing space in a room while connected to one or more rectangles.

Help the parents of your church to connect with their kids in meaningful ways. They already look to you as the expert, so exercise your expertise and teach them to become a vital part of your ministry. The only way parents can connect with their kids on spiritual matters is to connect on general topics throughout the week. Help show them the powerful message of putting down their phones and talking to the family or turning off the TV and opening up a board game. Get them to help their child with homework or sit and read as the child does homework. What high school student enjoys doing algebra while Dad or Mom watches TV, and what younger child loves reviewing spelling words while Dad and Mom enjoy a movie together?

You're right. The parents in your church may not be able to help with calculus, but they can read the math text with their child or show support by sitting nearby reading another book. If the student plays an instrument, teach parents to share their practice time by listening or again reading while they practice. Parents can also assist with drills on any sport in which their child is involved—they do not have to be experts at the sport, but they need to be in there trying.

When adding fractions, you simplify the denominators by making them the same and then add the numerators together. If the church gets only one hour of spiritual influence each week, what number do parents get to shape their own kids' spiritual growth? Add the two numbers and grow the spiritual influence. What is interesting is how this strengthens parents as much as it does the kids.

Church leaders can show parents how to connect. This will reverse the way they think, because the typical parents bring their kids to church to be taught Scripture. They have been conditioned to do this in sports, education, and music—take them to the experts, who will teach their kids while Dad and Mom cheer from the sidelines. But what they don't realize is that their kids would greatly benefit if Dad or Mom took on a portion of that role themselves. It is not that parents do not want to be involved; they just do not know how or do not feel capable of helping. This is where church leaders should shift some attention away from the children, teens, and preschoolers and toward the parents of those same age groups. By providing more opportunities for parents to influence the kids, church leaders can help increase the numerator of influence.

No, parents do not get all of the other 167 hours of our original fraction, but they do have influence during key times like commutes, meals, and evenings at home. Since parents are the major shapers of character, values, and behavior, you need to recruit them. Get dads and moms involved at home to reinforce the lessons from church. Do not let them pass the kids' spiritual development off to you alone. Instead, help them learn and work with you to disciple their kids. They need to learn how to manage the rectangles, increase conversations, and invest in teachable moments. Remember: Kids interpret the world through their parents' cues—the church helps the parents act and react for their kid's correct interpretation. This describes the power of generational discipleship. Today, it starts at church and continues in the home. But one day, it will begin at home and overflow into the church. D6 parents are your ministry multipliers!

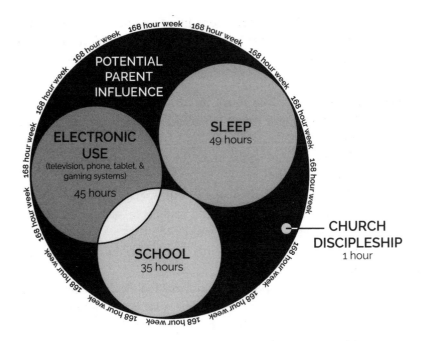

D6 Connection

Questions to Ask Yourself and Ministry Leaders

Look at the Venn diagram and see how little overlap the church has on a kid. Now ask yourself and your team the following questions:

- What portion of the diagram has the greatest amount of influence on our kids?
- In which segment is the church spending our efforts, budget, and time?
- Is it time to shift our efforts to include coaching parents to help us in this process?
- What tools can we put in the hands of parents to help them feel confident to connect spiritually with their kids?
- What are key benchmarks or milestones in a child's life when parents need the most coaching?

■ What would our church look like if we got thirty to forty percent of our parents involved in the spiritual development of
their kids?

Questions to Ask Parents in Your Church

■ How much of a sports fan could you be watching only one
hour of ESPN each week?

■ Do you feel that media and personal electronics could be the
new drug of choice?

■ I know you care about the health, social, and career choices
your child makes. How would you like to be more involved in
the faith value choices of your child?

■ Where can you carve out time in your schedule just to connect
and talk?

■ How long can you go without your mobile device before your
head rotates to look for it (not because you are afraid of losing
it, but because your hand has begun to twitch)?

■ If your kids take their cues from you, can you show less importance to the mobile devices when at home and in the company
of your family?

■ Have you found ways to allow your mobile device to help interact with their kids and Scripture?

■ In what ways could you talk about your small group, life group
lesson, and your child's lesson more than once each week?

Resources

Shift by Brian Haynes (milestones for ministry leaders)

Legacy Path by Brain Haynes (milestones for parents)

52 Creative Family Time Experiences by Timothy Smith

Parenting Teens by Richard Ross and David Booth

D6 2nd Generation Curriculum

D6 Family App

D6 Devotional Study Guides for each family member

3 D6 Goes Beyond Deuteronomy 6

Passing on a legacy of biblical faith to the next generation has always been part of God's plan.[1]
—Brian Haynes

It started when my kids began to play soccer around first and second grades. I coached their recreational teams for eleven years. They played right up through high school, and each served as the captain of their school's varsity team. Every year, first-time players appeared on my roster. But both novices and soccer veterans need to work on basic drills like passing and dribbling at both practice and home, so I assigned practical exercises for all the players to do at home.

Strengthen the Weak Side

It was easy to spot the kids whose parents worked to help the player's development when not at a practice or game. As a coach, I had a saying, "The difference between a good soccer player and a great soccer player is the use of the weak-side foot." Anyone can kick hard and accurately with his or her right foot when right hand dominant. The only way to get better is to work at home, kicking repetitively with the weak-side foot.

Almost every soccer player wants and needs a parent watching practice, playing with them at home, and being an active part of the sports experience. And the same, of course, is true for church involvement. Ministry leaders could develop another saying: "The difference between a good ministry and a great ministry is the use of the weak-side parents." And it takes just as much effort to develop and hone the parents in your congregation as it does to develop that weak-side foot. No matter the quality of the coach or youth pastor, parental involvement makes a huge difference to the child.

Generational Discipleship in Scripture

God spoke about the power of generational discipleship not only in Deuteronomy 6, but throughout Scripture. He began making His intention clear at the time of creation, when He told Adam and Eve to "Be fruitful and multiply and fill the earth" (Gen. 1:28). If you believe that command was limited to physical procreation, then you will not understand why He had to repeat it. As noted in the genealogies found in Genesis 5, the earth grew very populated, and yet God showed His disappointment in this "multiplied" people because they were not following Him. The flood allowed a do-over, and God spoke to Noah's family, saying again, "Be fruitful" (Gen. 9:1, 7). It seems clear that the essence of His intent was *multiply My presence on this earth through your children.*

Watch the generational thread wind its way throughout the Old and New Testaments. God told the patriarch Abraham, father of the nation of Israel, that he should direct his children and family in righteousness and justice (Gen. 18:19). Moses instructed the family leaders to be able to answer their children's questions by showing how God's involvement in everyday life has purpose and meaning (Deut. 6:20-25). In Isaiah 38:19, seven hundred years later, Hezekiah described how each generation will define God's greatness based upon what the previous one has taught.

After the fall of Judah and Israel, God still focused on generations passing along their faith and values during the rebuilding of Jerusalem. The great leader and contractor of the wall, Nehemiah, worked quickly to complete his building project, but called a time-out to talk to the leaders of the families. When the wall was half-built and the enemy was threatening and mocking their God, he said, "Do not be afraid of them. Remember the Lord, who is great and awesome, and fight for your brothers, your sons, your daughters, your wives, and your homes" (Neh. 4:14). What a powerful command for us today!

Next, note the transition from Old to New Testaments as the family theme flows seamlessly through every age. The Old Testament closes with a generational exclamation point in Malachi 4:6, showing God's desire to turn the hearts of the fathers to be in tune with their children and vice versa so each will follow God. Interestingly, events of the New Testament opens with Elizabeth hearing what John the Baptist, her future son, would do. Luke 1:17 describes how he will "turn the hearts of the fathers to the children." The principles of generational discipleship appear consistently throughout Scripture for all people. And they still apply to us today—even if we have, like the generations of Nehemiah, forgotten to be our kids' spiritual leaders.

The New Testament quotes Deuteronomy, Psalms, and Isaiah more than any other books in the Old Testament.[2] Jesus quoted from the twin pillars of Deuteronomy 6:5 and Leviticus 19:18, summarizing them into two commands[3, 4]: "And he said to him, "You shall love the Lord your God with all your heart and with all your soul and with all your mind. This is the great and first commandment. And a second is like it: You shall love your neighbor as yourself. On these two commandments depend all the Law and the Prophets" (Matt. 22:37-40). To suggest Deuteronomy is outdated or limit it to ancient Israel would overlook how often the words of Jesus, Paul, and the New Testament as a whole reference this foundational book in general and this passage in particular.

From Generation to Generation

Church leaders must constantly look for better ways to equip parents so they, in turn, can coach their kids. The D6 philosophy comes from ancient roots found in the way God instructed Hebrew parents to be leaders in their kids' lives. From the very beginning, God wanted the tabernacle, and later the temple, to be the center of life around which people built their homes (or pitched their tents). Homes or tents surrounded the tabernacle in distinct fan-like sections according to their tribes, indicating that when God moves the church, the people respond by moving as well.

God's intent has always been a close-knit church leading and parents teaching one generation after another. The core Deuteronomy 6 passage shows parents how to allow their love for God and His Word to overflow into the lives of their kids and let a Christ-following relationship be caught and taught:

> Now this is the commandment—the statutes and the rules— that the LORD your God commanded me to teach you, that you may do them in the land to which you are going over, to possess it, that you may fear the LORD your God, you and your son and your son's son, by keeping all his statutes and his commandments, which I command you, all the days of your life, and that your days may be long. Hear therefore, O Israel, and be careful to do them, that it may go well with you, and that you may multiply greatly, as the LORD, the God of your fathers, has promised you, in a land flowing with milk and honey.
>
> **Hear, O Israel: The LORD our God, the Lord is one. You shall love the LORD your God with all your heart and with all your soul and with all your might. And these words that I command you today shall be on your heart. You shall teach them diligently to your children, and shall talk of them when you sit in your house, and when you walk by the way, and when you lie down, and when you rise.** You shall bind them as a sign on your hand, and they shall be as frontlets between your eyes. You shall write them on the doorposts of your house and on your gates.
>
> Deuteronomy 6:1-9 (emphasis on verses 4-7)

This passage shares God's *command*, not suggestion. God intended it to describe an educational process for families to disciple each generation. Deuteronomy 6 instructed the entire nation about how their faith and values could reach their great-grandchildren. These few verses shaped the lineage of Israel and still have the ability to shape our culture today. At heart, this command tells us that we are to love God, love His

Word, and teach our kids to do the same. The best lessons come from natural interactions during everyday life, much the way Jesus used parables to teach His disciples. D6 or Deuteronomy 6 asks parents to look for teachable moments throughout the day to help their kids adopt and own what they model as adults.

Reciprocal Relationships

The New Testament sibling passage to Deuteronomy 6 is Ephesians 6, and the parallels are stunning. Paul begins this chapter with additional commentary on the commandment to honor your father and mother. In recalling the Ten Commandments that were so familiar to New Testament believers, Paul noted that the command to obey your parents requires a reciprocal relationship. Dads and moms expect honor, respect, and obedience from children. But Paul reminded parents, specifically dads, that to receive honor, they must likewise be careful not to consistently agitate or anger their kids, but carefully nurture a relationship.

Tim Kimmel, known as the grace-based parenting guy, defines grace as "God's love showing itself in relational determination."[5] The church should teach parents how to intentionally build relationships filled with grace. Dads provide a model for kids, who often derive their view of the heavenly Father by what they know and experience with their earthly father. Deuteronomy 6 and Ephesians 6 expect dads (and moms) to build healthy relationships with their children and teens.

The Ephesians passage also discusses critical issues for family relationships. Paul taught the New Testament believers a code of conduct for the home where the relational connections emanate from emotional ties, and anger issues push kids farther from the parents and from the heavenly Father.[6] Paul spoke of parental anger and how it can discourage kids in Ephesians 4:29, 5:17-18 as well as in Colossians 3:20-21.

The church should help parents recognize that the heavenly Father loans their children to them for a season. Like good stewards, parents must increase their kids' self-worth to line up with their actual worth as God determines it. Parents cannot go about this process alone, but will need the help of the church and some specific individuals such as lead pastors, children's ministers, youth ministers, grandparents, aunts, uncles, and other special people who will champion and reinforce the biblical teachings through godly relationships.

The Three Chairs

Bruce Wilkinson, author and founder of Walk Thru the Bible Ministries, shared a powerful message called "The Three Chairs" that describes well the generational impact found throughout Scripture. The famous passage in which Joshua declares that he and his house will serve the Lord appears in Joshua 24, just before his death. Verse 31 of the same chapter shows the next generation who outlived Joshua and knew about God's works among the nation of Israel. But flip a few pages ahead in your Bible to find Judges 2:10, the spiritually fatal phrase. There arose another generation that had no clue who God was or what He had done.

This adds up to three generations or, as Bruce describes it, three chairs. The first chair is the generation who knows God intimately and experiences His work in their lives. The second generation or chair knows about God from hearing their parents talk about Him, but they have not dived too deeply in their own personal walk. The third chair does not know God at all and cannot be considered a Christ-follower.[7]

There are other examples of the three chairs such as Abraham, Isaac, and Jacob, where we see a lie from the first chair (Abraham) modeled for the second chair (Isaac) until Abraham's grandson sitting in the third chair (Jacob) is known for his deceptive ways. Look at David who fell for Bathsheba, Solomon who fell for many, and then Rehoboam, who split the kingdom in a wicked fashion. From the first generation to the third, each had a different view of God; commitment turned to compromise and finally to confusion. The thread moves from a Joshua-type commitment to grandchildren who are confused about why anyone would claim a biblical creator and a God who is trustworthy.

Bruce later connects three more characteristics of the three chairs with Revelation 3. He describes the first chair as putting people first, the second puts pleasure first, and the third focuses on possessions. The church at Laodicea was rich, but Christ called them poor and said, "I wish you were either hot (first chair) or cold (third chair), but because you are lukewarm (second chair), you are leading the next generation away from me" (Rev. 3:15-17, paraphrased). In fact, Christ Himself felt like the outsider at His second-chair church as He stood knocking on their door, longing for them to live in a first-chair relationship.[8]

Generational Connections

In 2 Timothy 3:14-17, Paul connected the reputation of the teacher to the validity of what is taught. This key passage emphasizes the inspiration of Scripture, but pay close attention to the surrounding verses. Paul told Timothy how, from early childhood, he had been well-instructed and prepared to represent the teachings of Scripture. Paul even pointed out to Timothy how his mom and grandmother shaped his early life, resulting in a godly heritage. Generations matter.

I detest reading the genealogies in the Bible. I use a phone app that daily reads Scripture to me, and hearing the genealogies makes them no more palatable. However, genealogies show trends, trajectories, and outliers. The endless list of people's names in a genealogy reveals the power of generational affects and effects. God uses people to influence culture and to create lasting cultural change.

The *Shema* of Deuteronomy 6 is named so from the Hebrew word for *summons*—"Hear, O Israel," or "Come listen to the Word of God." The commands were both propositional in that they affirmed who God is and personal in how each generation was to be committed to Him.[9] Dr. Elmer Towns was speaking at a conference and revealed how teachers throughout our lives were knowledgeable, but what made one or two of them most memorable were the relationship connections that inspired us to want to learn.[10] This demonstrates what both Deuteronomy and Ephesians teach about the way instruction and influence come from your closest relationships, those people who believe in you and help connect the biblical lessons with everyday life.

You cannot limit D6 to a cultural setting found only among the Israelites and only in the Old Testament. The model of the family shows up everywhere. God the Father consistently refers to believers as His children. He is the Father, the church is the bride of Christ, and He adopted us into His family. Relationships become the structure upon which instruction, discipleship, and growth can occur. We are called to make disciples—a person dedicated to follow a person (Christ) or teaching (Scripture) and this call begins with our family. Our Father follows the same pattern: He seeks a close relationship with His children, whom He does not agitate or anger but seeks to rescue and redeem.

Without a relationship, one limits potential influence and teaching. Each of the three synoptic gospels (Matthew, Mark, and Luke) show Jesus quoting the *Shema*, but Mark uses the word *ek* (the Greek preposition "with") reading it as "with all your heart," which suggests we should pursue God with our entire being—with our heart, soul, mind, and strength.[11] And not only do the writers of both Old and New Testaments address generational discipleship, but Christ's way of engaging life reveals it as well. Remember when He reminded the disciples of the value of allowing time with the children in the midst of the busy ministry day? These examples clearly show us that D6 extends well beyond Deuteronomy 6. Generational discipleship is proclaimed throughout Scripture as a pattern, a standard, and a challenge.

D6 Connection

Questions

- What are some "weak-side" tendencies that need intentional effort both in helping at church and home? (work done at home like players who work hard apart from games and practice)
- In light of Abraham, Isaac, and Jacob heritage principles, can you list some traits you have because of your parents and grandparents?
- Now flip that question and list areas inherited that you wish to change.
- At times believers move back and forth between the first and second chair. Which chair are you sitting in? Where are your children sitting?

■ Do you and your families in your church look for ways to be the Heavenly Father to your children? List some ways dads and moms blow it and ways they reinforce it.

Resources

Experiencing Spiritual Breakthroughs (Kindle Edition) by Dr. Bruce H. Wilkerson

Deuteronomy 6 in 3D by Garnett Reid

4

Biblical Worldviews and Battleships

*The value of decisions made without deliberations
determines your worldview.*[1] —Ron Hunter Jr.

Why do rocks sink while massive steel battleships float? Barges carry enormous amounts of cargo on top of the water, and yet a wedding ring dropped in a lake sinks right to the bottom.

Have you ever skipped rocks across a pond? With a slight side-arm motion and a flip of your wrist, you allow the smooth stone to roll off your pointer finger as its flat surface strikes the water. After four or five bounces and skips, it finally submerges, never to surface again.

Of course, you want to help parents launch their kids more like battleships and less like those skipping-but-sinking stones. But how?

Shipshape

What does it take to make a battleship float, much less cruise, to its destination, fighting battles along the way while sustaining itself through every nautical mile? The technical term is *displacement*. Modern metal battleships did not exist in the third century BC, but that is when Archimedes, a Greek mathematician and engineer, first used this term.[2] It refers to the phenomenon that explains how objects—whose weight seems to defy gravity—float on bodies of water.

Simply put, displacement occurs when the object weighs less than the water it displaces or moves. The displaced water pushes back up and keeps the object floating. Google "displacement activities" and have fun with your kids learning and being amazed together.

We have already discussed the importance of correcting the flawed fractions, of helping parents see the importance of their involvement in their kids' spiritual growth. So how do you help them ensure that their child, like the battleship, displaces enough of his or her surroundings to stay afloat? Now, go further. Is floating really the goal? Or do parents want their sons and daughters to have the power to chart a course, cut through the waves of life, and fight any battles needed?

The United States calls its military the "defense industry" even though battalions, squadrons, and fleets are assembled to fight—an offensive posture. In fact, the great hope of a nation is to build a capable fighting force in hopes it will never be used, but if called upon, will have no doubt of victory.

In terms of helping parents raise their kids, the best defense is also a great offense: helping them give their kids a biblical worldview. This involves theology, apologetics, philosophy, and other foundational components, but I prefer to describe the process as building a battleship. It's not a perfect illustration, but constructing such a ship describes the role of parenting with the goal of launching children as self-sustaining, capable people, ready to navigate the ongoing issues of life.

Worldview Defined

To help understand what a biblical worldview is, we should take time to grab a working definition of the word *worldview*. A great definition is "the fundamental perspective from which one addresses every issue of life."[3] A more descriptive definition suggests a worldview is "a set of mental categories arising from deeply lived experience which essentially determines how a person understands, feels, and responds in action to what he or she perceives of the surrounding world and the riddles it presents."[4] Guba showed how a basic set of beliefs determines one's actions.[5] David Naugle, one of the leading worldview experts, shows how a worldview causes a person to possess an unconscious intellect.[6]

Put all of these definitions together and add the adjective "biblical," and you'll discover how a worldview provides a person with the unconscious intellectual ability to make decisions, render value judgments, and form opinions based upon principles of Scripture without deliberation. This second-nature way of responding, or *biblical worldview*, provides a reliable guide when facing uncharted waters.

How does the church equip parents to give their kids a strong, biblical worldview of battleship proportions? It exists not only to help parents build their kids' battleship designs, but to become an integral part of the construction process. Parents incorporate what the church teaches into coachable moments that frame the child's biblical worldview.

Building Battleships

What aspects should a church focus on to help parents launch teens into the vast ocean of life? How should we build these young battleships? We can borrow a page from Bloom's Taxonomy to help achieve our goals. Here, we find six steps to learning: knowledge, comprehension, application, analysis, synthesis, and evaluation.[7] Christian publishers through the sixties, seventies, and eighties taught the stories of Scripture again and again. Their approach conditioned parents into defining success as their children coming home from church and repeating what they had learned in class. But this only represents step one or two on Bloom's chart: the ability to recall, summarize, and explain the principle. In order to produce lasting impact, you want to go higher.

Many churches take families into the obvious areas of application, but at this point, they are only halfway up the steps of learning. A person on the fourth step will analyze, distinguish, diagram, and test the principle. The fifth step shows an ability to connect with other similar experiences, reconstruct, and even devise a plan based on this learning.

Did you ever have a teacher who inspired you to love history? If you answered "*No!*," your teacher probably never got past the first two levels of Bloom's Taxonomy, asking you to memorize dates and events. If you answered "*Yes!*," he or she helped you see connections with other events and the cause and effect of various happenings.

For example, the effect of the storm that sank much of the Spanish Armada changed England's future and thus all of North America's history. The invention of the railroad created rapid expansion during the industrial age, similar to the way the Internet connected nations and commerce. One can trace a domino effect on events, and a great history teacher shares *why* and *how* rather than just *what* and *when*. And so does a great Bible curriculum, teacher, and parent.

All that is good, but we must strive for more. The final step (and the overall goal of learning) is to defend what one has learned by assessing with an appropriate type of discrimination and estimation that discerns qualities. Only when a church's discipleship plan intentionally charts each age toward climbing all six levels of Bloom's can you suggest that those who have progressed through this program are ready to launch and sail. By ensuring your curriculum or lessons implement Bloom's Taxonomy of learning, you will excite and equip students in ways simple knowledge and memorization cannot.

Back to the Basics

We can return to the battleship illustration to learn more about the goal of building a biblical worldview. We tend to think only of the guns found on the battleship or destroyer, but of course, we need much more than firepower to create a formidable vessel. Other characteristics of a solid battleship include a mess (kitchen and dining area) to sustain the feeding of the sailors, a medical bay to mend and assist in healing, communications areas for interaction, and areas for the many other everyday life-sustaining necessities. No ship sails alone; its strength lies in being part of the fleet. Teach families the need for each other, the church as a whole, and the body of Christ. Show them how we help each other heal, grow, and interrelate, all the while recruiting more people to serve.

Building a biblical worldview comes from remembering the goal found in the root definition of worldview. *We must build within our kids the ability to make wise decisions unconsciously.* Because they have already considered the principles many times, they have no need to think things through. To achieve this ability, learners in each age group, from grade school on up, should constantly climb the six steps of learning. Lessons should walk the student to the top. And the church should teach learners to make this climb so often that it occurs naturally and without the need to stop and plan or consider.

One of the flaws in this battleship illustration lies in its implication of a completion to the building process. But worldviews are always being shaped, sometimes for good, and at other times under negative influences. Anything that influences a person's thinking to affect behavior is a worldview shaper. The church is one of the shapers; others include parents, books, education, mentors, the Internet, television, songs, art, icons, and many others.

And remember, our core illustration works well because of displacement: the ability to help people be in the world but displace that which is "unhealthy" or "sinks us" (Romans 12:1-2), to defend and battle, and to have a purpose and direction. The church must work to encourage and train parents to help build their kids into buoyant battleships and to help other parents do the same. No more skipping rocks or dropping things of value and allowing them to sink to the bottom. Help your church's parents build great battleships by learning to instill a biblical worldview, and you'll launch powerful ships for generations to come.

D6
Connection

Questions

How do you know if your church is helping parents equip their kids to have a biblical worldview? Examine your programs. Are they teaching kids and teens to:

- Recognize the authority of Scripture?
- Know the stories of Scripture?
- Memorize principle passages of Scripture?
- Know how to filter decisions through Scripture?
  - Likes and dislikes
  - Attitudes

- ° Relationships
- ° Habits and disciplines
- ° Goals
- ■ Find answers on their own from Scripture?
- ■ Think critically about information?
- ■ Understand how science and history complement Scripture?
- ■ Persevere through the challenges of life?
- ■ Discover and use their God-given talents and gifts?
- ■ Build their children and grandchildren one day?

Resources

Teaching Students Not Lessons by Jonathan Thigpen

D6 2nd Generation Curriculum (teaches biblical worldview on age-appropriate levels every week from whichever passage or topic is being studied)

Apologetics for a New Generation: A Biblical and Culturally Relevant Approach to Talking About God by Sean McDowell

77 FAQs About God and the Bible: Your Toughest Questions Answered (The McDowell Apologetics Library) by Josh McDowell & Sean McDowell

The Questions Christians Hope No One Will Ask (With Answers) by Mark Mittelberg

The Reason for God: Belief in the Age of Skepticism by Timothy Keller

Holman's Christian Apologetics Bible

The Apologetics Study Bible for Students by Sean McDowell

Rite of Passage Parenting: Four Essential Experiences to Equip Your Kids for Life by Walker Moore

5 The One-Eared Mickey Mouse

Parents are the primary teachers in their children's lives, even if they don't know it.[1]—Timothy Paul Jones

How did Adam Smith and Henry Ford alter the way churches do ministry? And how does Mickey Mouse help you understand it?

Division of Labor

It all started with a famous Scottish economist, Adam Smith, who in 1776 wrote a book entitled *Wealth of Nations*. He advocated a theory dating back to Plato, the "division of labor," which helped business owners become wealthy. He used a story about a pinmaker to explain the theory. It goes like this: A pinmaker who makes metal pins could make between one and twenty pins in a single day, depending on his skill. The completed pin takes multiple steps. Smith theorized that putting a person in charge of one or two of these steps would help proficiency. One person unspools the wire, the next straightens it, the third cuts it, the fourth creates a point on it, the fifth fattens it for a head, and each step or two after this has a person in charge, up to the eighteen distinct operational steps to create a pin.

How does the owner of the pin factory afford more employees? One pinmaker could make at best twenty pins per day. But ten efficient workers, each performing one or two of these tasks better than anyone, else produced *twelve pounds* of pins per day. Each pound contained four thousand pins, bringing the daily total of those ten men to 48,000 pins per day.[2]

Fast-forward from 1776 to 1913, when Henry Ford changed auto manufacturing from twelve hours per car to two hours and thirty minutes by using a moving assembly line. Ford wanted to make the Model T affordable to the average person. He continued to study efficiency, expertise, and production. He dissected the manufacturing process of the Model T down to eighty-four distinct steps and trained the Ford assembly workers to excel at just one of them. Starting production in 1908, Henry Ford built 15,000,000 cars by 1915 in a way that would have made Adam Smith proud.[3]

So where does Mickey Mouse come into the picture?

Mickey Mouse Ministry

It took a few decades for business savvy to carry over into the church, but many still remember when the first hire made by a growing church shifted from associate pastor to youth pastor. Eventually, the church started looking at the specialization of ministry leaders. Seminaries were producing well-trained youth ministers, wise churches were hiring them, and youth groups became the focal point for attracting families. Adults were excited to have a leader who could communicate with their teenagers at last. The youth minister was given a large room with great liberty to paint it in crazy colors, add couches, contemporary music, and later, video games. Youth groups were never cooler!

The adults wanted the youth group to be a part of the church, but on the perimeter or fringe of the rest of the congregation. If you graphed the look of the youth ministry as part of the larger church, it would look like a small circle barely touching the perimeter of the larger circle. Stuart Cummings-Bond described this as the "one-eared Mickey Mouse."[4]

ONE-EARED MICKEY MOUSE

The senior adult ministry discovered the youth group's organizational setup and added another ear to the mouse. Later, leadership would add children's ministry, preschool ministry, and college or young adults, all on the outer rim of the congregation. Each ministry functioned on its own and had its own activities, curriculum, and budget, so things got a bit competitive. And the addition and growth of each ear provided an unintended consequence as the church lost its collective identity. You see, it was a really big deal to move up to the children's ministry, and kids couldn't wait to finally make it to the youth group. But no one wanted to leave the coolness of the youth ministry and enter the adult service. That gap was the widest, and this transition ended up as the place where the church lost the most people.

Mind the Gaps!

If you have ever ridden the public subway or trains in a large city, you remember hearing the recorded safety message played in the terminals—"Mind the gaps!" The voice warns about the danger of stepping into the six-inch gap between the train door and the platform. Many who failed to pay attention were hurt, twisting their ankles, breaking their legs, or worse. This recorded announcement started in 1969 in the underground subway systems in London, but it should have sounded for the next decade in the churches—"Mind the gaps! You lose them between children and teens and certainly between teens and adults! Mind the gaps!"

Another great advantage to the church hiring seminary-trained youth leaders was that the teens had never had someone who could speak their language about spiritual areas of life. The church still needs this expertise, but on the inside of the circle and not on the perimeter. The multiple ears on our Mickey Mouse should not look and act like separate teams but teammates on one team.

Yes, the church still needs ministries geared to youth, children, pre-schoolers (yes, ministry, not babysitting—this age group is capable of far more), young adults, adults, and senior adults. There is tremendous value in working with the seasons of life, but spiritual life does not end when segueing to the next season. The youth group should not be so cool that Dad and Mom cannot compete and stop trying. The youth minister should not position the parent as uncool and out of touch, nor should the adult church be presented in the same light.

In fact, the mark of any successful ministry leader is when those who have moved up to the next age ministry thrive and grow even more than before in their walk with Christ. So my message to you for genera-tional ministry success is this: mind the gaps!

ALL EARS INSIDE THE CHURCH

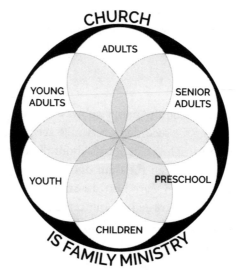

A Team Approach

So how do you bring distinct age-segmented ministries into the circle of the whole church without dissolving their value or misplacing any leader? The key is orientation. The ministry leader (youth, children, etc.) shifts the focus from one perspective to three. The one-eared Mickey Mouse ministry leader will only focus on those within the age group, for example, the youth minister focuses only on the youth—after all, that is what the title describes. But by bringing the ear inside the circle of the church, the orientation of the youth minister shifts to include more than one group, the other ministry leaders, and the parents of the youth (see graphic, All Ears Inside the Church). The wise youth minister recognizes the value of providing leadership by helping the youth transition to adults who still love God and want to be part of His church. Staff members and volunteers have up to six years to help the youth make this transition, and going it alone would not be wise.

Imagine an intentional handoff with overlap between children and teens and between teens and adults (or young adults). Once per month or quarter, the youth minister and children's minister could trade places in speaking to the specific age groups and help prepare them for the shift by inspiring the future transitions.

Now contemplate the exponential power of that same youth ministry building intentionally on what the children's ministry started and involving the parents each step of the way. It would also be great to involve the lead pastor in this rotation to start developing relationships. But don't make the mistake of thinking this paragraph is only about leaders speaking to the various age groups, or you'll miss the power of building relationships and making heart-connections. Don't look on these as speaking gigs, but heart gigs.

The next set of followers and leaders is the parents of the age group to which you are tasked to minister. They will follow you almost anywhere if you teach them how to connect with their kids and give them the tools to win.

You spend a lot of time preparing for the hour or hour and a half you have to influence your students—not as much as you want to spend, but every week, you pray your lesson sticks. What would happen if your students' parents helped continue to teach that lesson when not at church? What would happen to the parent who becomes the teacher at home and the student who sees his or her dad or mom leading—yes, even modeling the same lesson?

If a single ministry can be the one ear on the lopsided Mickey Mouse called church, then ministry leaders must recognize that church can be the lone, small ear on your out-of-kilter life. This further illustrates how church can become the 1/168 isolated amount of time on the fringes of anyone's week—kind of tacked on, but never in the center.

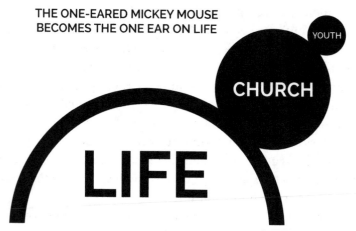

THE ONE-EARED MICKEY MOUSE
BECOMES THE ONE EAR ON LIFE

YOUTH

CHURCH

LIFE

Let's position church as the influential center of life. And let's bring the ears inside the circle and play on the same team. Prepare to hand off the student—not keep their loyalty. Expect the next age level to take the student higher and keep investing to make that happen. Put your ministry where your D6 heart is.

D₆ Connection

Questions

Instead of questions to help you review this chapter, I have an exercise for you. Do this alone or (preferably) with your fellow staff and volunteers.

Take a blank sheet of paper, turn it landscape, and list each ministry age (as your church delineates them) across the upper middle of the paper. List each ministry from youngest to oldest. This may be by class or departments. Look at the diagram below for an example. You are creating a chart similar to the one below, but it reflects your church.

DISCIPLESHIP THAT HELPS CHURCH & HOME
more than one hour a week

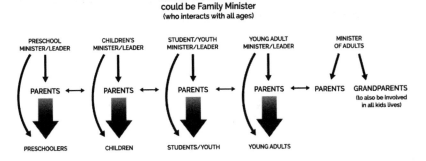

*if possible, minister to parents even if not in church to be involved with kids at home

- How can youth leaders capture the hearts of children and pastors capture the hearts of teens?
- How can each ministry leader spend more time with parents (even if they are not in church)?

Now, think about and discuss (if possible) what your church can do to connect the class or department leaders/teachers of each age to the parents. Remember, parents have the most influence on their kids (represented by the larger arrows) and spending time helping them spiritually influence their kids will be the best use of part of every leaders time. Challenge each LifeGroup, small group, or Sunday School leader to spend nearly as much time helping the parents of their class or group as they do teaching their group. Divide their time and watch the results multiply.

Division of labor works in the factory, not in the church, and silos—stand-alone storage areas shaped like large standing tubes—are only effective on the farm. Now, get rid of those isolated ministries and bring them back to one purpose and one mission, all working toward the same end. The Bible says He is the God of Abraham, Isaac, **and** Jacob—three generations, not one.

A key component of this reorganization can be found in chapter 7, "Staffing for a D6 Church."

Resources

Family Ministry Field Guide: How Your Church Can Equip Parents to Make Disciples by Timothy Paul Jones

6 The Senior Pastor Complex

I think we forget that the most important thing to our kids is to show up in their lives.[1]—Leneita Fix

The title of this section may have piqued your curiosity like the tabloid headlines. And moving the word *complex* to different positions drastically changes what you are about to read. The *Complex* Senior Pastor would not be an easy chapter to write. Move the word again, and it sounds like a place for older people: The Senior *Complex* Pastor. The chapter with the actual title is no easier to write, but my prayer is that it will free pastors and other leaders to lead, cast vision, and work hard in the D6 initiative.

Heroes or Hypocrites?

During the first two years of the D6 Conference, one of the most frequent questions from very talented staff members was, "How do we get our pastor on board with a family emphasis?" Several of those asking this question had tears in their eyes. Staff members long to have their pastor leading this charge because they know the influence of the one who communicates from the pulpit each week. Children's and youth pastors immediately see the value of developing generational gladiators, but too often, their commander is absent from training, leading, and fighting.

The truth is that numerous senior pastors wish they could be the gladiators leading the charge, but they feel disqualified. They also feel passionately torn as they share how they have watched their son or daughter grow up and walk away from God.

The departure may have happened when their kids questioned their faith as professors pushed them further away by adding more doubt. Or their son or daughter may have made one mistake that took them down a drastically different path than expected. Yes, the parents themselves may have exacerbated the issue over embarrassment or not knowing how to deal with the situation. None of this was intentional. All of it was painful.

No matter what, distraught feelings over their perceived failures cause pastors to want to warn and help others but, at the same time, fear hypocrisy. Having encountered variations of this issue so many times, I concluded that they have a hard time championing what they feel they have not lived or done well for fear of a lack of credibility.

Pastors and Prodigals

Most of these pastors have real integrity. They can be trusted with the most sensitive details when leading a counseling session and would never think of hurting anyone intentionally. The fact that lead pastors have dedicated their entire lives to helping people should speak for itself. Each staff member, regardless of past mistakes, can find the grace and direction to help others. If you are a pastor in this situation, your deep desire to help other parents may, in fact, move you to address the hang-ups that are holding you back. There is hope and a way for every staff member to help lead this charge and advocate for an involved family ministry.

I realize this chapter may be a painful read. Because of its subject matter, I've tried to write it in as straightforward a manner as possible. If you are a parent of a prodigal or a child whom you fear is making choices that are leading them toward a prodigal experience, you will want to take extra care to ensure a close friend and/or ministry partner reads it alongside you for encouragement and discussion.

Remember, you are not alone. A recent Barna study shows that thirty-three percent of pastors say their child or children are no longer active in church. You may feel having a child like this presents a conflict of interest or showstopper when leading family ministry. But the same Barna report lists the top reasons why pastors believe their kids struggle with their faith:

- 28%—Unrealistic expectations others place on them
- 18%—Exposure to negative aspects of the church
- 17%—Pastor is too busy for them
- 14%—Faith is not modeled consistently at home
- 9%—Worldly influencers or peers
- 7%—Self-discovery and free will, resulting in rebellion
- 7%—Failure to make their faith their own[2]

You should know that I, too, have battled these emotions. When I did not feel like the dad my daughter needed during her high school years, I wondered how I could champion D6. She wrestled with decisions related to whom she hung around and who had influence over her heart. Those four years were long for my wife and me, and we felt as though our walk through this period might never end. Only God's grace allowed us to keep a close relationship with our daughter the entire time. She did not need me talking about the topic each time we were together. We sought a normal relationship through experiences that kept us close: shopping together, Starbucks runs, doing an art-project together, and just showing up for events in her world. This kept our hearts connected even when our minds thought differently about certain subjects. When or if you draw a line in the sand over an action, then you draw a line separating your relationship. She told me more than once, "daddy, I already know what you are going to say and saying it again will hurt more than help." She knew I had not compromised on the issue when staying quiet, but it kept us connected. I heard a wise friend and former teen editor for Randall House advising another parent, before we had teenagers, "do you want to die on this hill?" That advice was filed away and became invaluable to me later and I would further counsel you: relationships should not change your rules, but rules should not trump relationships. And although our daughter is in a great place now, not everyone can make such a claim about their child. Your feelings, like ours, are understandable. Recognize that even negative emotions can be harnessed into helping others reach their kids early and figure out ways to attempt reconnecting with your own as a model to others who need similar help.

Leave the Guilt Behind

Guilt is an unwelcome emotion that directs a Christ-follower away from sin, but also makes them feel disqualified from doing what is right. The latter applies in what I call the senior pastor complex, where Satan uses the emotion of failure or perceived failure to prevent effective ministry in key areas.

How many topics do you preach on or encourage people in where you consider yourself an expert? Some pastors are gifted in sharing the gospel in their personal lives and never meet a stranger. I know one church planter who goes to the hardware store every week for the sole purpose of outreach and has a way of getting at least one or more families to attend his church that week. That is a gift! But not everyone can easily talk to strangers, and yet none of us are exempt from evangelism.

Our lack of expertise in carrying out a particular scriptural command does not disqualify us from working at it or even from teaching others about it. Guilt causes us to stop trying, ignore, or digress to another action—even in family ministry where it matters most.

Satan often uses emotions to sideline some of the greats who could make a huge difference in any of Christ's causes. C. S. Lewis's classic book *The Screwtape Letters* shows how Satan's greatest tactic is not the big sins but the small ways he makes us feel inadequate and unfit.[3] How many dads have you met who feel like the perfect father with no regrets? *None!* And moms have the same struggles, pouring their all into their kids and still dealing with inadequacy as they watch their children make mistakes.

God gave Adam and Eve a chance to follow or disobey Him in the Garden of Eden. He does not force us to love or obey Him any more than earthly parents can with our children. This means following our heavenly Father's model is most helpful, as He has never given up even when His children do not turn out the right way.

As a leader, how would you advise any church member who feels guilt, shame, or failure in an area of his or her life? If you were counseling someone experiencing any of these issues, would you forever sideline this person from ever being used in any position of the church? I think not. I believe you would share the descriptive definition: "Guilt ignored and unconfessed makes you the warden over your own imprisonment."

Another principle you would share with hurting parents is this one: "There is nothing so bad that God cannot forgive or handle." Paul intentionally killed Christians, David slept with his friend's wife and later murdered the friend, and Peter denied knowing Christ. All of these and many others throughout Scripture found forgiveness, and later in life, God used them in great ways.

You are not disqualified from family ministry; you just need to deal with your guilt and get back in the game. What if a couple who struggled in their marriage could end up as one of your greatest set of mentors to younger couples? You would advise them to admit their shortcomings, stop ignoring that area of their lives, educate themselves with Scripture, books, and conferences (or counseling if needed) to help them face the issues. You would help them prepare, and when they were ready, you would give them opportunity to turn this negative into a positive.

It is time to take your own advice.

Own the Past

Some of you have raised your families with wisdom like Solomon. Your insight was spot-on. Your knowledge was there. You modeled the illustrations of Proverbs, "My son, hear me, stay away from, steer clear of, avoid . . . ." Nevertheless, somehow, like Solomon's, your kids strayed away.

While we find great wisdom in the book of Proverbs and its sayings, principles, and promises, we also have Ecclesiastes. This book is a reflection written by a father with the benefit of hindsight at the end of his life. You may have preached with the wisdom of Solomon, but now you identify with the dad in Ecclesiastes and wish you could do it again—differently.

The people in any church know all too well what happens in the pastor's home. If you really want to know about the families in your church, teach their children in life groups, Sunday School, small groups, or kids' worship. Whether in prayer time or routine discussions, the honesty of little ones just tells you what Dad and Mom are doing. While teenagers become more guarded in classes, they are rarely anything but transparent in social media. And rest assured that the youth group knows reputations, good and bad. If people already know what is happening in your home, refusing to talk about it will not make it less real. It will, however, make you seem less honest.

One of the marks of a healthy church is authenticity from the staff and lead pastor. You have no idea how refreshing it is for the people to hear that you, their senior pastor, struggle with temptation, feel guilt, have a marriage that needs work just like everyone else's, and may not have been the ideal parent. Your people realize that mistakes provide prime learning experiences. Most test-takers will say that after getting back the graded copies, they remember the answers they got wrong more than those that were right. That knowledge helps them prepare for the final exam or coach others taking the same class. Admit what your people already know and use this first step to help them avoid the same mistakes.

Educate Yourself

So how do you work toward a biblical do-over? You can prepare, or you can recover. Of course, preparation brings better results when it is adequate. Just as when you were in school, if you bomb the first test, an A in the course is highly unlikely. While you cannot redo the past, you can recover and work toward making the future a better encounter. Most students who do not do as well on a test as they had hoped will study harder to get ready for the next one. You can read from Scripture passages dealing with parenting and watch for each place the heavenly Father interacts with His children. The Old Testament is filled with numerous case studies. The New Testament also shows Christ's reaction to His disciples' disappointing actions.

Learning more in this area provides two positive results: you get to help others and you also find opportunities to reconnect with your own children and grandchildren (at home or grown). By attending a conference, reading a book, or finding a mentor in the area of family ministry, your newfound information creates a reason to share. You can tell your congregation how much you wished you had learned this when you became a parent or when dealing with certain seasons of the parenting journey. They will understand that your newfound knowledge came from a sincere discovery to help them be better parents while also working hard on your continuing journey.

In 2013, my wife was diagnosed with cancer. Both of us already knew about this disease and had helped people in our congregations work through their treatments. But the moment cancer enters your immediate home, you become an amateur expert, reading and learning everything you can to help fight this monster. Treat any separation between you and your kids like a cancer. You should become the imperfect expert at finding ways to reestablish a relationship on mutual terms, not just your own. Realize that, as with cancer, you do not always win the battle, but you want to do everything within your power to increase your odds.

Ask Forgiveness

If your child is not walking as close to Christ as you desire and you feel guilty, you may need to ask forgiveness from either two or three sources. After reading all you can on the topic of prodigals as well as the portions of Scripture dealing with family and the role of parents, you must first ask God to forgive you. God our Father demonstrates the role of a parent to us with high expectations, great involvement in our lives, and a high level of patience and coaching when we fall short. He teaches more about how to relate to Him than perform for Him.

The second source of forgiveness is your child. I know, you are thinking, "He (or she) is the one who walked away from this relationship." You have been committed and faithful to God. You have always worked hard, never missed church, and the list of justifications goes as far as you need to temporarily ease the pain. You may have been the ideal parent but lost your child to a disorder, peer influence of your child's friend, or substance abuse, and your heart is broken without personal fault.

Whatever the case, the most important way to heal is to begin the restoration process. You will need to own the blame to begin tearing down the wall even if you feel it is more your child's or someone else's fault—so adjust or edit the following to your own words and situation. Go to your son or daughter and say something like this:

While I have not always shown it, I love you more than you know. Recently, I have been reading about how many ministers have worked hard, have been successful in growing the church or ministry, and yet have lost one of the most important relationships in the world—the one with their child.

I am so very sorry. I put _____ before you. I spent more time _____ rather than having long conversations discussing what matters to you. I did not have answers for you about _____.

I know at times I made you feel our problems were all about you when I, too, contributed to this situation. I cannot change the past, but I am owning it. I would give anything to go back and do things differently. While I cannot go back in time, I can try to change what I do in the future. Will you forgive me? Will you let me try to start rebuilding our relationship without guilt, without one-sided expectations, without preaching to you, and just work hard on communicating, loving, and getting back to listening to you?

If you are willing, I would like to earn back your trust and your confidence, I hope and pray that we can just find each other all over again. I am sorry—can we try again, because you mean so much to me?

If you mean these words and change the way you interact, refusing to operate with your adult kids or isolated teenager from a controlling heavy hand or guilt-imposed set of tactics, you may be amazed at how close you will become. And only a close, authentic relationship will allow you, over time, to speak into your kids' worlds.

The third level of forgiveness applies only to certain situations. When your child fits into the first four categories of Barna's research listed on page 45 (unrealistic expectations others place on them; exposure to negative aspects of the church; pastor is too busy for them; faith is not modeled consistently at home),[4] you may need to seek forgiveness from your church leadership and even your church body as a whole. Yes, they already know about the problems, but your admission and their act of forgiveness opens the channels for future ministry.

Before taking this decision to the church, discuss it with core leaders and accountability partners. Who knows? Your own modeling of humility and the proper steps of restoration may begin a new era among your church families. Which would you prefer: a pastoral legacy of guilt and secrecy, or one of humility, transparency, and reconciliation?

Don't Pretend to Be the Expert

The delicate balance needed shows a lead pastor championing, but not pretending. Talk with your staff and your church about the goals and benefits of building a strong family ministry. Again, the combination of a leader's vulnerability in sharing scriptural truth along with a brokenness over what should have been true encourages others in a powerful way.

Move forward from your own pain to helping parents in your congregation avoid your mistakes. The congregation puts so much stock and trust in the lead pastor—they need a champion. The staff needs a champion. The parents in the congregation who have also struggled need a lead pastor providing the next steps for reaching their grown children. No one is asking you to fake anything. After failure, people can improve at anything.

Michael Jordan, five-time MVP (Most Valuable Player) of the NBA (National Basketball Association) and arguably one of the greatest basketball players ever to live, said, "I've missed 9,000 shots in my career. I've lost almost 300 games. Twenty-six times, I've been trusted to take the game-winning shot and I have missed. I've failed over and over and over again in my life." Then he added, "That's why I succeed."[5]

Michael was a great player because he worked hard at it. He disappointed plenty of people, and yet he used his misses to get better. Help other parents who feel like disappointments and failures find ways to strengthen the relationship with their kids. This may be one of the most important missions you and your church can accomplish.

Vision-Casting

People learn from models who have raised their kids well and from those who have not. The lead pastor provides the healthiest motivation for parents and grandparents who listen each week. I can tell you that parents whose children are not serving God or, worse yet, denying God or living in open sin, grieve to the point that it consumes them. Dads of such kids find self-inebriation by working harder or longer hours. While this may have been one of the original contributing factors, it's all they may know to do. Moms may mourn to the point of a broken heart, which often interferes with their marriage relationships. Most will not talk openly about this for fear of being judged—just like the complex borne by senior pastors.

In your quest to learn how to reconnect with your kids, you will have discovered the reasons why kids walk away from church and their faith. Those hurting parents feel as alone as you—and it is time you stopped pretending your prodigals do not exist. Help the other parents stop doing what has not worked such as badgering, guilting, or even ignoring their kids. Study the topic of prodigals and make good notes; weave this wisdom into your sermons, your communications, and your staff meetings.

Or better yet, model the priority of the family and make sure you are not always available to the church. As Dennis Rainey said so well, "Your legacy through your children is more important than the legacy of your ministry through your church."[6] Become an encourager to other parents—start a connection study group committed to learning more, praying together, and coveting to break this cycle. Cast vision so others will learn how to relate with their kids from your experience, your study, and the abiding witness of Scripture.

The Importance of the Senior Pastor in Church Initiatives

Until an initiative is important to the pastor, it will most likely remain unimportant to the church as a whole. Just as kids take their cues from parents, parishioners take theirs from their pastor. Lead pastors and other staff members who have earned the title *leader* will find people desire to accomplish what you deem significant. When you describe in visionary terms the critical nature of family ministry, parents will begin to learn, just as you have, how to reconnect with their kids.

Pastors have helped many people battling guilt from their past. God forgives pastors just like anyone else. But, just as doctors make the worst patients, pastors are often the worst counseling recipients. It is time to get past any complex you have over your kids and start helping to prevent others from similar paths. Any guilt should guide you to change, not imprison you to stay the same. Lead pastors simply cannot sit this one out.

Trust God to do His part while you work to stay connected with your child. We have the book of Ecclesiastes to assist us in keeping others from repeating Solomon's mistakes, including the poor relationships he had with his family and others. Consider preaching a sermon or series of sermons from Ecclesiastes. Be vulnerable in the pulpit. Share your mistakes and challenge others not to make the same ones. This could be the most powerful preaching you will ever do.

D6 Connection

Questions

- How many and who in your church lives with the consuming concern of their child not being on a godly path?
- What resources can the church provide to come alongside these parents to encourage and equip them?
- What steps are most important for the church to take to reduce the future percentage of prodigals?
- Can you identify and help plan steps toward reconciliation: first of relationships and alternately toward godly reconnects?
- Read closely the "Helping Parents Dive Deep" chapter of this book and use these principles to help parents connect to their kids and adult kids on a deeper level.

Resources

Grace Based Parenting by Dr. Tim Kimmel

Why Christian Kids Rebel: Trading Heartache for Hope by Dr. Tim Kimmel

Engaging Today's Prodigal: Clear Thinking, New approaches, and Reasons for Hope by Carol Barnier

The Pastor's Family by Brian and Cara Croft

When They Turn Away: Drawing Your Adult Child Back to Christ by Rob Rienow

It Starts at Home by Kurt Bruner and Steven Stroope

https://www.barna.org/barna-update/family-kids/644-prodigal-pastor-kids-fact-or-fiction#.VO_rr7PF8wx

7 Staffing for a D6 Church

*Don't succumb to excuses. Go back to the job of
making the corrections and forming the habits that
will make your goal possible.*[1]—Vince Lombardi

Fantasy sports leagues transform the normal sports fan to a fanatic on steroids—ouch, did I just use that metaphor? But where else can you draft a team that you would rather watch play than the actual ones on TV today? What would it look like if you could build your ministry staff the way you built your fantasy team? What if we could throw all the best youth ministers, children's ministers, and so on into one big pool?

I am chuckling as I write, considering the possibilities. Over the past almost-decade, because of the D6 Conference speakers, I have met, talked with, learned from, and become friends with many of those I would consider a *Who's Who* list of talented ministry leaders. I could select quite a dream team from among the list, even though it would be hard considering the talent among that pool. And if you are one of those speakers and friends—then *yes*, of course I picked you over all the others.

More than Talent

The above exercise is what every pastor goes through when hiring a new staff member. The thoughts of getting an all-star youth minister makes one almost salivate in a spiritual lustful sort of way. But ask yourself these questions: When has it ever been true that if you have the best talent you can be assured you will win all or most of your games? And how many times have you witnessed the best talent with poor execution?

Often the difference between a team of talented players and a winning team is a great coach. The coach determines preparation, the playbook, and the expected cultural attitude. A pastor is the head coach and the adhesive that holds the team together. And like the coach, the pastor should not be expected to be the entire team, even when no paid staff exists.

February 1, 2015 in Glendale, Arizona will be forever discussed in the annals of Super Bowl history. With twenty-six seconds on the clock, second down and one yard to go, it happened—what most refer to as the worst play call in history. Instead of running the ball (with the leading back averaging six yards a carry), the Seahawks called a pass play. The Patriot's cornerback Malcolm Butler jumped the route and picked off the ball, stealing a sure victory from the Seahawks.

But in Seahawks' head coach Pete Carroll's postgame interview, he blamed neither the receiver nor the quarterback. Instead, he readily admitted, "There's really no one to blame but me."[2] The best talent in any sport or part of any ministry team rises and falls on the collective effort of the team. However, no one can discount the play calls that cast the team's direction and vision. And these plays cascade from the head coach, referred to in a church setting as the lead pastor.

The Followership Principle

Your church is either structured so the leadership team makes decisions or so the congregation helps decide or even votes on most major items. Either way, wise leadership cannot ignore the power of the principle of followership. Bad decisions and poor execution will cause followers to lose interest, commitment, and ultimately stop participating, regardless of who makes the call.

Many pastors who work under a congregational governing system bemoan the lack of authority to do what is needed. But in those instances, the pastor is seeking power and not leadership, which do not always coincide. Leadership inspires, models, and serves the followers, but power can be selfishly motivated and exercised without regard to the needs of the followers. When people are inspired, they want to follow, a different posture than being obligated to follow because of power or titles. In other words, inspiration and leadership need no titles. Instead, they gather power proportionate to the motivation the leader instills in the followers.

Staff or Volunteers?

Likewise, your church either has paid staff or works with volunteer leadership. Do not create an identity complex if you have little or no staff. Whether you have a large staff or no staff, the effectiveness of ministry rises and falls on the development of volunteers. (If you have no hired staff or limited staff, then every time you read "children's minister" [or any other staff position] in this book and you do not have one, insert the words "children's leader" or champion for whoever comes from your volunteers.)

As the head coach or pastor, you can draft your talent either from a volunteer group of members or by hiring the next staff member. Think about the principles of the draft in ministry terms. The departments or ministry teams that most need talent should get priority. Wise selection means you look for people with the skills and passion to fill the position. When you draft a person, you train him or her.

Something else to consider is that on draft day, each player in the NFL (National Football League) gets a team jersey with his name on the back as cameras snap photos capturing the moment. Do you celebrate your volunteers, or do they feel like the last person picked to do what no one else would do?

Drafted Volunteers Become Team Members

Lead pastors should make volunteers feel like part of the team, not employees or grunts. I talked with a tremendous leader and pastor who said one of his church's values is excellence every Sunday that honors God and attracts others. This church, like a number of others, call its volunteers the Dream Team and constantly reminds them they are part of the team that makes the dream happen.

This pastor also takes one Sunday each year to celebrate volunteers and give them gift cards to coffeehouses, ice cream shops, and movie theaters. Praising those who serve also creates a recruitment opportunity, so he uses this window to ask others to join the team, telling them, "We have a place for you."[3] This truly reinforces the principle that says the way you get people is the way you keep people.

This wise pastor went on to explain that finding a great team does not stop with one Sunday a year, but is built into the every-week mindset. He made it a point to say that when he shares sermon illustrations, he makes sure the heroes in the story are not ministry leadership, but volunteers who make a difference. Work hard to cultivate a strong volunteer base regardless of how small or large your paid staff.

Help People Find Their Place

In addition to drafting new talent, you also can rearrange the talent you have to become what you want. God does not equip all people equally, but He does equip all people. Leaders help each person find not only their God-given individual gift, but also where to use it.

Let's face it: some people do not need to be in the choir or sing "specials" (that word is so abused) no matter how often they tell you God has laid a song on their heart. Equally wrong is the person capable of ushering, teaching, greeting, or stacking chairs who watches from the sidelines. Help believers discover their place to serve and help them develop.

Some ministry leaders have the gift of recognizing talent in others, while others use simple gifts assessments to assist in this process. Most ministry leaders cannot get to know everyone on the same level, so allowing people to assess their gifts and record their top five areas will also allow others to recruit from the results. This tool can be attached to new member classes or get-acquainted groups and helps that person know up front that this church intends to help them become an active part of the body. By helping new members quickly get to know the culture of the church, you will be assisting in their assimilation and encouraging them to become serving members rather than served members.

Move People to the Right Spot

There are a few questions to ask yourself often that help you gain a different perspective when planning and retooling ministries within your church. The word *ministry* below can refer to any component of the church, such as the youth, women's, or children's department, or to the church as a whole.

- If this ministry went away, would anyone in the church or community really miss it?
- If I were starting this ministry all over again, what should it really look like?
- What is the purpose of this ministry as distinct from other ministries?

The honest answers to these questions help build objectivity and a focus on ministering to people more than perpetuating programs. The next step is to help your volunteer or staff team answer these questions and see if they reach similar conclusions or insights. It is always easier to launch something new, change something old, or kill a ministry when you have other influencers who see it the way you do.

Asking the second question from this list may help you evaluate your staff or volunteers in a better light. The person who was once ideal to lead a certain area or serve on that team may have grown or come through a different season of life and be a better fit somewhere else. You are not looking to mix things up unless it makes sense—but rearranging talent can provide huge boosts in multiple ways. A change in team members can provide fresh sets of eyes on that ministry, new dynamics and relationships, and extra energy to work hard.

For assigned team members on your staff, making a move can be difficult but rewarding. Just look at the coaching decisions surrounding blue-chip recruit coming out of high school ranked #2 safety in the nation as he began his college football career in 2011. Starting only once for the Florida State Seminoles in 2012, Karlos Williams played back-up safety during all of the 2011 and 2012 seasons, but began serving as kick return specialist in his sophomore year. Two weeks into the season of his junior year, 2013, Coach Jimbo Fisher moved Karlos to running back during the second game, where his first career carry resulted in a sixty-five-yard touchdown.

Transferring from defense to offense is not common, but that move created a high-impact player for Florida State. You may remember the National Championship Game between FSU and Auburn where on the fourth down with four to go just before the half, the fake punt found Karlos carrying the ball for what may have been the most important seven yards of his career. This pivotal play is credited with creating the momentum that helped Florida State win another national championship—all because the coach dared to make a major move with the team.[4]

Building a D6 Organizational Chart

You cannot overlook the power of the pulpit to cast vision, set the tone, and help create the church culture. Richard Ross, who has devoted his entire life to youth ministry, wrote a book targeted to senior pastors because, as he so clearly indicates, the transformation of a youth ministry or family ministry cannot be the work of a staff member alone. Ross describes how adults are the true spiritual and positive influencers on teenagers, but many are spiritually lethargic, and the senior pastor has the biggest influence on this group. He goes on to state his case:

> The youth pastor can and should have a role in the spiritual transformation of parents and volunteer leaders. But the senior pastor must take the lead role, and he has to know specifically how that role should look.

He goes on to say,

> Some of the most needed alterations in youth ministry involve systemic change that will ripple through the entire congregation. Even the brightest and most influential youth pastor cannot lead such change alone. The active engagement of the senior pastor absolutely is essential.[5]

The point of this discussion is that no matter what your organization chart looks like, the lead pastor's role must be one of helping mobilize the adults, parents, and grandparents in this D6 cultural change. If the senior pastor feels disqualified because of prodigal-leaning kids, review the previous chapter on "The Senior Pastor Complex." Transformation cannot happen without the lead pastor leading the charge.

Many people find organizational charts distasteful, but the lines do create distinct responsibilities and lines of serving. Notice I did not say lines create boundaries, because we are all working together. Each of the charts you will find here are designed only to illustrate the basics of the goal. You can replace any position with paid staff or volunteers based upon where your church is in this journey. Many churches accomplish D6 ministry very well with all volunteers. Revisit Chapter 5, "The One-Eared Mickey Mouse" to see the silo affect in which a ministry stands alone, and note the organizational chart below that resembles this disconnected culture.

Standard Chart

This standard chart works in a church without staff as long as the pastor actively coordinates the efforts of each age ministry to be D6 and not siloed (stuck off in its own isolated tower). It also works in a staff church if the lead pastor is the family ministry champion and works to coordinate the efforts of every ministry to complement the other. However, the vast range of pastoral duties often requires time spent in relationships, strategy, and sermon prep, leaving little legitimate room to coordinate family ministry.

STANDARD or TYPICAL
Organizational Chart

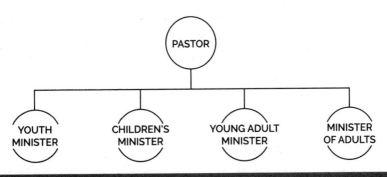

Family Minister Chart

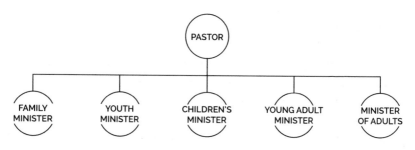

FAMILY MINISTER WITH NO LEADERSHIP CHANNELS
Organizational Chart

If the pastor catches the family vision, rather than upset the dynamics of the team, the pastor may choose to create another staff position at the same level as the others. This produces the "Family Minister with No Leadership Channels Organizational Chart" shown above, which prevents the coordination of all the ages of the church into the kind of true generational effectiveness that is the goal of D6 ministry. The family minister needs to help the transitions between ages, the coordination of materials being taught and watch for ways to build on the previous age groups succession. Therefore, the family minister needs a leadership role over other ages of ministry.

Another dysfunction of staff alignment happens when the family minister, discipleship minister, next gen pastor, or whatever title the church uses for this position, coordinates all ages except adults. The following shows that silos still appear in this Almost Family Ministry Organizational Chart.

Almost Family Ministry

The intentions of the next organization chart are well-meaning, but fall short of coordinating all ages of the church into one generational discipleship culture. After all, are not adults moms and dads? Are they not also grandparents? That's family, and they need coordination to minister together in "generational discipleship." It's not younger generational discipleship. Take a look at the Almost Family Ministry Organizational Chart for both staff situation and volunteers. Note the role of serving to connect all ages.

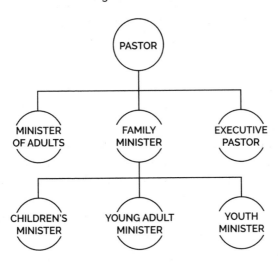

ALMOST FAMILY MINISTRY
Organizational Chart

D6 Family Chart

In the D6 Family Oriented Organizational Chart with staff scenario, the lead pastor and the family minister are on the same page. The lead pastor champions family ministry regularly from the pulpit, and the family pastor coordinates efforts among all ages to ensure church and home connectivity.

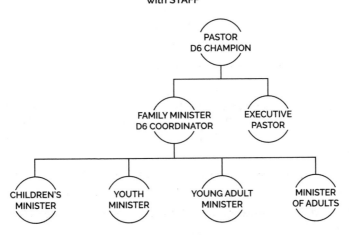

D6 FAMILY ORIENTED
Organizational Chart
with STAFF

The culture of the church creates weekly opportunities for parents and grandparents to connect and then become the coaches at home for the kids and grandkids. With the two key leaders working together, the staff understands how to develop an intentional church and home strategy.

D6 Family With Volunteer Chart

Any of these organization charts could have the family minister, discipleship minister, or next gen pastor serving in two places if done objectively. For example, the family minister might also serve as the minister of adults or youth minister as long as this position has oversight over all ages rather than a peer level relationship. While not ideal, this arrangement can help overcome a budget issue. Ask yourself, "How much time in our staff meetings centers around the Sunday morning service only or around what happens only at church?" If the percentage is high, you are putting most of your eggs in the one-hour basket. You have been reinforcing the flawed fraction 1/168 rather than using your ministry multipliers. How much time do you spend helping parents cultivate opportunities to maximize portions of the other 168 hours? Organizational charts are not the solution—they do, however, provide a structure for implementing the solution.

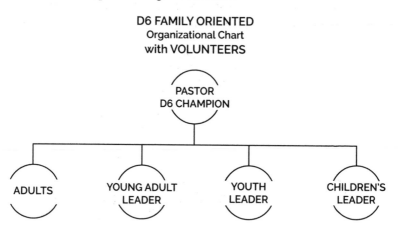

If you are the lone pastor or have only one staff member, the preceding chart may describe your church. As pastor and adult leader, you will oversee volunteers who fill the roles of youth leader, children's leader, and young adult leader. I cannot include enough organization charts to portray every possible scenario. But the principle of avoiding the creation of silos will create one D6 champion, and that person may be the coordinator. If you have one staff member, he or she should be trained to be the coordinator, but not the champion. The senior pastor should always take the role of champion.

Distinguishing Your Culture

To prevent the one-eared Mickey Mouse from reoccurring, you will need to establish a culture that defines and guides the attitude and action of all the leaders within the church, paid or voluntary. I have had the benefit, like many of you, of traveling to other countries. When I get that opportunity, I like to get away from the touristy part of the cities and venture back to see how people live, the grocery stores where they shop, and the local eating spots. Finding a place to sit and just watch people helps you begin to observe the true culture.

Almost every group has a unique culture that defines it, from people who drive Volvos to those who ride Harleys and those who use Macs to those who do not. Watch the advertisements for any area of the world, and you begin to grasp what their culture is like, similar to the way certain sponsors on TV shows indicate a particular demographic or psychographic. When you see commercials advertising diapers, minivans, and the greatest tote bags ever, you know the program you are watching is designed for young moms. Inversely, if you see ads for reverse mortgages, awnings for your patio, and prostate supplements then you can bet the majority of the watchers are men over sixty.

In any case, the key question for you as a staff member or lead pastor is this: "What do guests and members define as the culture of your church or your ministry?" You have one—you just need to know it, embrace it, or redefine it. This redefinition begins with the leadership and is caught by everyone else over time. What ministry leadership emphasizes and models will, over time, cascade down to the congregation to form a culture.

The late, legendary Dean Smith, who coached the University of North Carolina from 1961-1997, created a whole new culture within basketball by working with the other coaches and leaders on his teams. Smith, who coached Michael Jordan in the early eighties, taught his players to value the whole play rather than just the score. After his players made a basket, he trained them to point to the guy who passed them the ball, thus honoring unselfish play. The Tar Heels Four Corners offense brought a whole new look on the court, providing an ingenious way to stall when in the lead in order to avoid running up the score. This play spurred the initiation of the shot clock. Coach Dean changed many aspects of the game, but the one cultural change that made him most proud was the graduation rate of his players: ninety-six point six percent.[6]

Grandparents, Your Secret Weapon

You call them Memaw, Papaw, Granddad, Grandmother, and other affectionate terms. This seasoned group often raises or has significant influence on their grandchildren and possibly on others in church as well. Some of the best batting coaches or offensive line coaches were former players. Using grandparents in ministry areas where they have previous experience is no different.

When it comes to family ministry, grandparents get it, especially the older ones. The younger grandparents do not perceive any possible imminent mortality. But the closer to death people believe they are, the more importance they place on what they do with their family. Limited time changes one's priorities.

Grandparents are typically good at dealing with people of all ages—even teenagers, in the right setting. Plugging these men and women into the right spots can be a big investment in the children's, youth, and especially young adult ministries. And what better marriage mentors could you find?

You may be thinking, "This could only work in smaller churches." If so, you could be robbing the value from both students and grandparents. Larger churches are finding this group of seasoned and wisdom-filled seniors indispensable. Older adults bring strength to the church, and by using them in strategic ways, [you honor them with value as they honor the church with support.] Help the older group want to help you lead the shift into a generational church.

Imagine what could happen in a young boy or girl's life if one of these grandparents identified a talent or skill and helped to develop it. Chap Clark writes about this very experience in *Youth Ministry in the 21st Century* (Baker Academic, 2015). He talks about someone spotting technical ability in a young boy and connecting that boy with the church's AV team to develop and nurture that gift. An attentive grandparent can initiate the conversation and help the youth minister link this student with both older and younger generations. Chap describes this adoption to show that it goes way beyond an older person spending time with a younger one. Instead, it involves the older mentor inviting the child or teen to become part of their world and share in a larger community.[7]

Generational connections help kids grant permission to adults to speak into their world. And when they do, the kids actually listen. As the senior adults work with the children's and youth ministries, some natural adoptions will occur as kids identify the seniors they wish to hang around. Cultivate the connections in which the senior adult is doing more than just teaching a lesson, but spends some time asking about the goals of that child and offering wise insight. Showing concern and being inquisitive will only open the door for them to give wise advice.

These senior adults get to keep on coaching, which proves beneficial for both sides. Connections like this are a healthy way to stretch the young person beyond their peers and into a world of healthy, mature, Christian adults who care for them. As with other goals in this book, intentionality is the key. Is it time to develop your secret weapon, grandparents?

A D6 Culture

Coach Vince Lombardi, the namesake for football's Super Bowl trophy, had a passionate way of teaching his players the basics. He was famous for grabbing the pigskin, holding it up, and telling his players, "Gentlemen, this is a football." Known for his tedious repetition of the basic skills, Lombardi also provided a depth of ingenuity and determination to make his teams strive to improve every year. He built his coaching staff and team to be the best at football.

Ministry leadership is not fantasy football—it is not even fantasy ministry, but you have the same possibilities to build and develop people to serve in key staff positions. No, you will not always get those you want, but go after those God has gifted, develop others, and shift people around—they will thank you later as it makes the whole church better.

You are the coach—what culture are you creating? Do your staff and volunteers understand its goals and how to pass it along?

Be cautious about trying to copy someone else's culture. Learn from leading churches—do not try to become them. Your community, people, staff, and opportunities are all different than from whom you learn. Prayerfully find the needs within the community in which God has placed your church. And never, ever forget what Scripture says about Christ's bride—the church.

Every pastor knows the basics (the non-negotiables), and how as the leader you build your team in such a way to follow the Great Commission and obey the Great Command. That is the overarching mission, and the way it looks in terms of programs and tactics will depend on how you bring your staff and volunteers to rally around or define your intentional D6 culture.

D6 Connection

Questions

- For fun, pretend you had a draft day and could choose from any paid or volunteers within your church to serve as leaders over any ministry and draft them on paper (then prayerfully consider if these should become a reality over time).
- Are you coaching your leaders, helping them develop and get better? If not what resources can you help them discover? (Some listed in this book would be a great place to start.)
- Does your church look siloed? Who coordinates all ages to complement each age department? How should your organi-

zational chart look to ensure family ministry is a higher priority?

- How effective are your seniors? DO you make them feel valuable and have you found ways to plug into their wisdom for younger generations in areas like marriage mentoring, teen coaching, or spiritually adopting kids (or young married couples) within the church?
- Do you have a senior ministry, self-centered and siloed, or do you have a grandparents ministry involved in children and youth ministry?

Resources

Family Ministry Field Guide: How Your Church Can Equip Parents to Make Disciples by Timothy Paul Jones

The Senior Pastor and the Reformation of Youth Ministry by Richard Ross

Leading From Your Strengths assessment tool – ministryinsights. com/leaders/leading-from-your-strengths-profile/

Spiritual Gifts tool – d6family.com/dna

Youth Ministry in the 21st Century: Five Views by Chap Clark, Fernando Arzola Jr., Greg Stier, Ron Hunter Jr., and Brian Cosby

Partnering with Parents in Youth Ministry: The Practical Guide to Today's Family-Based Youth Ministry by Jim Burns and Mark DeVries

ReThink by Steven Wright

Sticky Faith by Dr. Kara E. Powell and Dr. Chap Clark

Great Lessons and Grand Blessings: Discover How Grandparents Can Inspire and Transform Their Grandchildren by Elmer L. and Ruth Towns

8 The Unseen Staff Member

Children do not reject our faith because of too much formal teaching; they reject it because we do not practice it.[1] —Sam Luce

In March of 2004, Michael Lewis released his book *Moneyball*, chronicling Oakland A's general manager Billy Bean's rebuild of the baseball team's roster. Not having the deep pinstriped pockets of the Yankees or the vast budget of Boston, how would the Athletics compete? The brilliance of the story, as millions now know from the movie released in 2011, came from recruiting under a new matrix. Watch the trailer to the movie[2] and notice the way the key question changes from "how to replace Giambi" to "how to get wins." Bean scouted players other teams overlooked because all-stars were overpriced and what mattered in a player was, "they got on base."

As noted in the previous chapter, churches should always seek to hire the very best staff member they can afford or recruit the most capable volunteers. Each leader, paid or volunteer, should strengthen a particular area of the church, causing the congregation to grow stronger. I could list the Derek Jeters, Jason Giambis, and Albert Pujols of youth ministers in America. Then I could also list the Mike Trouts, Andrew McCutchens, and David Ortizes of children's ministers. Like the baseball all-stars, they are few in number, and each is truly worth every penny. So let us look at the one staff member every church can afford and should hire.

This staff member will not require an office, does not complain, has great ideas, connects well with people of all ages, disciples better than anyone, and will mentor your entire teaching staff. This staff member is curriculum.

Before you stop reading, recognize the trends have changed more than once. There was a time when churches bought their entire curriculum from the denominational publishing house matching the church's affiliation. The next step came when independent publishers offered more attractive-looking teen curriculum, and churches bought curriculum from multiple places. All this occurred when the overriding perspective of ministry leaders and parents was that the church held the sole responsibility for the spiritual development of the home. Chapter 2, "1/168—Flawed Fraction or Ministry Multiplier?" explains why this goal was flawed from the start.

At about the same time, some of the larger churches decided to write their own curriculum in youth and children's areas. Churches of all sizes often allowed the adult classes to do whatever they wanted, including teaching only from the Bible without a curriculum. Let's examine each of these options and its implications.

Buying From Independent Publishers

Overall, denominational publishers in the seventies, eighties, and even into the nineties produced curriculum that only taught the stories of the Bible through the first two to three steps of Bloom's Taxonomy (review Chapter 4, "Biblical Worldviews and Battleships"). Much of the curriculum produced during those same decades lacked creativity, excellence, application, and information to help teachers. This opened the door for independent or para-church publishers to enter an anemic sector and fill a gap.

The independent publishers' goals began with providing artwork and illustrations that were more current, attractive artwork, teacher-friendly instructions, and up-to-date applications—all much-needed! They delivered it, and churches gobbled it up. The secondary goal was to produce denominationally neutral curriculum. But what most people remain unaware of is the hot list these publishers used to produce their curriculum content. It compiled words, topics, and doctrines to avoid so the curriculum would not reflect any specific denomination. The major topics on their list that never make it to the curriculum include such important points of doctrine as salvation, the Holy Spirit, and hell. The independent publishers thus concentrate on the topics described as low-hanging fruit. While this approach is popular, the omissions are rarely noticed until after the churches that use them lose depth and any distinct doctrinal integrity. A generation can go by before you notice the loss.

Buying From Multiple Sources

Buying from multiple sources has both strengths and weaknesses. The strengths are obvious and explain why you might choose this option. You want to provide the very best curriculum for a particular age group, which pushes you to a variety of publishers. The downside can cause parents to be overwhelmed when each child brings home a different lesson, story, and take-home paper. See the diagram below of a typical Sunday as each age studies great stuff (adults study 1 Corinthians, young adults study The Beatitudes, students or youth study the fruit of the Spirit, children study David and Goliath while preschool tackles Abraham and Isaac). All these different lessons and silos reinforce the problem of not just a one-eared Mickey Mouse but this example shows something worse, five-ears on Mickey! Dads and moms, new believers, or long time church members who may not be familiar with the many stories of Scripture, will have trouble keeping up. If you are reaching new people, they will not be familiar with the most common stories of Scripture. When their kids ask them questions from two or three different sections of the Bible, the parents get overwhelmed and send the kids back to the church for all the answers. This perpetuates the problem of "it's not the parent's responsibility."

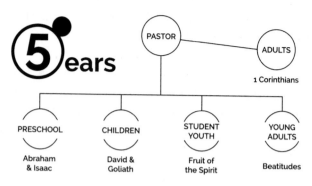

EACH MINISTRY IS ONE EAR
doing their own program

If you do not believe this, just go to any minivan in your church parking lot and ask to see their back floorboard, where you will find the past three weeks of take-home papers. Parents feel inadequate to carry on conversations with their kids and simply do not try, missing the exponential teaching they could use to reinforce what happens at church.

Buying From a Single Source

How different could it work if each age studied the same family theme so when the kids come to dad or mom, they just had the same lesson. Parents can keep D6 going throughout the week, when the kids get up, go to school, come home, eat dinner, and go to bed. Teachable moments occur even in new believers homes. It would look something like this:

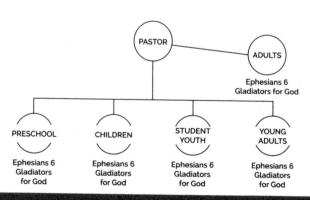

D6 FAMILY WAY OF TEACHING
with seperate classes but one theme

Staff Members Write Curriculum

Churches now have access to some of the most qualified children's ministers and youth ministers ever because of the high-quality programs offered by seminaries. Those who have not attended seminary also find better training than in the past due to the availability of high-quality books. Having high capacity leaders is most desirable, but how you use their equipping is a matter of wisdom.

Some churches have tasked or allowed staff to write curriculum. The most often-stated reason for writing curriculum is, "I have not found one that is exactly what we need." The problem comes from the fact that no one likes all parts of any curriculum, not even the one written by the staff member. However, because they love the staff member, the volunteers typically cannot or do not complain.

Most curriculum takes more than one person to write, edit, and design effectively, but assuming one staff member can do it, a wise leader will ask if that is the best use of his or her time. Any decent teacher can make a poor curriculum come to life in the classroom and inversely, poor teachers take life from an effective curriculum. If a staff member creates an ideal curriculum, the definition of *ideal* applies only to the one who created it. The moment teachers receive it, they must adjust it to their classrooms and students. The problem the staff member/writer attempted to solve is still present, but the staff member has spent an inordinate amount of time on this project. For the most part, a staff member's time is better spent developing people, not curriculum.

Staff members find the greatest return on investment when they intentionally build into other people. Imagine more time spent developing and mentoring students, teachers, and volunteers. Every minute used in developing others pays major dividends as your skills now span across more areas. Take the average percentage of time used to produce curriculum out of your schedule (and those of others involved) each week and determine how much money is being spent. The formula looks like this: total number of production hours (writing, editing, designing, duplicating) multiplied by the hourly rate paid to those involved plus the cost per copies. This number is your weekly cost. Now, multiply this number by the number of weeks the curriculum is used.

A hypothetical example would look like this: 20 hours a week times $20 hour (that stipulates a youth pastor being paid at a low salary of $42,000 a year [20 x 20 = $400]), and done over fifty-two weeks would cost $21,000. A church often feels that if a check is not written, the project does not cost anything. But this homegrown curriculum may be costing far more than you realize. And for large churches that have each department writing, wow, you do the math. Buying a curriculum and adapting it the same way teachers do with staff-written curriculum may make curriculum your least expensive staff member and allow your other staff members to invest their time where the dividends are greater: people.

The No-Curriculum Choice

The practice of not using any curriculum is most often characteristic of youth pastors and senior adults—for completely different reasons. Youth pastors who teach classes often do not want to be restricted to a thirteen-week type of curriculum and end up creating their own unique lesson each week. They often move around from one topic to another. The content is rich and solid, and the topics selected may provide diversity and balance across needed areas.

Senior adults do not use curriculum for the opposite reason: they want to take as much time as needed in a particular book of the Bible. It is not uncommon to find senior adults spending a year or longer studying just one book. When asked how long they like to spend studying a topic or a book, the answers come quickly: "As long as it takes."

There are two problems with the seniors' perpetual-study approach. The biggest issue comes from the fact that no guest wants to jump into a yearlong study three to six months after it has started. This group of students becomes what is known as a closed class, meaning the membership is the same as the teacher had two years ago and will have two years from now minus any deaths.

The second concern comes from the inaccuracy of the claim, "teaching only from the Bible," when the teacher consults various commentaries, books, or even the Internet. Who knows how closely the resources consulted match up with the doctrinal statement of the church?

Rarely are such issues monitored, until in three to five years this trend produces a new set of beliefs from one of the most important and financially supportive groups in the church—the adults.

In addition, the problem with any teacher who jumps around or stays for extended periods of time in a particular book comes from a lack of balance. Ignoring what I have learned from studying spiritual formation and Christian education for nearly thirty years, if I did not use a curriculum, I would lead my class through my personal favorites. And that is the tendency of anyone (youth minister, senior adult teacher, or someone else) who teaches without curriculum. My selections would start with the book of Nehemiah (and take a year to do so), then move to select epistles by Paul like Galatians through Philippians, add the book of James, and rotate one of the Gospels into the mix along with the book of Genesis. Your list might look different from mine, but you, too, would leave out the bulk of God's Word.

The best way to illustrate this error is to watch an unsupervised child eating from a buffet line. The child loads up on mac and cheese, mashed potatoes, and chocolate cake while intentionally overlooking vegetables and proteins. You need to take students through more than the highlights of Scripture whether they are your own favorites or an overly simplistic two-year scope and sequence. Students of all ages should crisscross through both Old and New Testaments on an age-appropriate level to see both the individual stories and the greater story of Scripture.

Curriculum, The Unseen Staff Member

Find a curriculum that works for teachers and enables parents to have wins at home. Putting everyone in the family on the same page makes parents feel comfortable talking through the lesson with their kids. They can typically field most of the questions because the parent's lesson is an adult-level teaching of the same weekly lesson. This alignment will revolutionize your discipleship, and multiple publishers offer this type of curriculum. Try it and watch how the intentional generational focus begins to revolutionize the discipleship in every age group.

Your church should not take a position such that, whether with a curriculum or without, the way you teach suggests discipleship happens *only* at church. Curriculum is not inexpensive, but for all ages, it is the best investment you can make. And it is the only item in your budget other than staff salaries that develops people.

Ask yourself how much money your church spends on coffee, toilet paper, napkins, paper towels, and similar items that while important, are less essential than the growth of your people. And watch the trends as more and more churches emphasize discipleship in smaller groups and classes. Providing a well-thought-out and developed curriculum accomplishes two major goals: discipleship of all ages and leadership development for teachers. A solid curriculum makes your teachers better, increases the maturity of your classes, and extends its ministry well beyond the one hour each week as it continues its work at home.

Hire the one unseen staff member that you pay no benefits, but returns a lifetime and generations of benefits. Pay for the best curriculum you can find that aligns families and complements the direction of your Deuteronomy 6 and Ephesians 6 goals. Just as Billy Bean changed the matrix for baseball, family ministry is changing the matrix for the church, and curriculum is the one place both small and large churches can equally compete and find success in connecting families.

D6 Connection

Questions

Ask these questions when evaluating a potential curriculum if a D6 emphasis is desired along with other advanced instructional goals (these go beyond the normal aesthetic evaluation):

- Does the curriculum provide an age-appropriate opportunity for all ages (at least grade school and above) to study the same biblical theme in their own classes?
- Does the curriculum offer a way for parents to know what all ages of the family are studying and provide a guide for inter-

action based on the lessons? (Both church and home components)

■ How long (in number of years) is the scope and sequence of the curriculum? (To cover a comprehensive understanding of the Bible)

■ Does the curriculum go beyond the cursory knowledge and application components of learning?

■ Does the curriculum offer at-home devotions to reinforce the lessons?

■ Does the curriculum intentionally help teach a biblical worldview?

■ Does the curriculum elevate Scripture as the authority for both faith and life issues?

■ Does our staff and leadership's view of curriculum further reinforce the myth that all Bible teaching should take place at church?

■ Does our staff work to develop people or curriculum?

Resources

D6 2nd Generation Curriculum—D6family.com

D6 Devotional Study Guides

D6 Family App

9 Reach and Teach Stragegy

Disciples are made one relationship at a time.[1]
—Dave Kinnaman

Is it more important to reach people or disciple them? The debate about whether to emphasize evangelism or discipleship has raged for decades, if not centuries. You can look at many churches and find pastors championing one side over the other, although they would never admit it.

Reach People

Reaching congregations tend to fall into one of two categories of either evangelism or outreach: the ones who reach their local community, and the ones who gravitate to global missions. Which of these areas is a strength for your church?

Ministry leaders' attitudes about outreach are vast. You find the pushy used car salesman type who wants to notch his gospel gun with one more win, and you encounter the quiet, personable type who builds relationships and attracts people to Christ. No matter where you fall, one inescapable reality about Christ's command to evangelize is that no one gets an exemption. Certain personality types may have a harder time connecting with strangers than others, but the command to go, to talk, and to share includes every Christ-follower.

You have read and heard about numerous methodologies of winning people to Christ, from drawing on a napkin to asking the right questions in a certain order. You have probably tried several along the way. Church outreach methods change as often as someone finds new success with another one. Each has been effective as the energy and people willing to use them. Make a list and count how many different methods you have heard about or tried. I hope you have not given up, because there is no earthly expiration date on the Great Commission.

While outreach programs have changed and will continue to do so, the one constant ingredient is relationships. You must connect with lost people over some topic, circumstance, and/or shared common ground. After all, people trust something new because of the one who recommends it. They try a new restaurant, a product, or recipe because someone they know or respect tells them about it. In marketing terms, this is called an endorsement. Having a high-profile celebrity or athlete endorse a product drastically increases sales—just ask Nike™. Billy Graham used the endorsement method by having major figures share their testimonies at his worldwide crusades.

But endorsements are not limited to people of celebrity status. In fact, you have strong recommendation power among the people around you. Your endorsement of Christ carries weight if they know, trust, and have a positive relationship with you. The book of John tells us about one of the lesser-known disciples. Not part of the inner circle of three, Andrew nonetheless introduces Peter to Christ. How differently would the Gospels read without his eagerness to endorse Jesus within the context of his relationship with his brother Peter?

Matthew, not the most outgoing among the disciples, hosted a gathering and invited friends for the sole purpose of introducing them to another of his guests, Christ. Who could forget Peter's famous reply to the invalid beggar: "I have no silver and gold, but what I do have I give to you. In the name of Jesus Christ of Nazareth, rise up and walk!" (Acts 3:6)? Peter did not know this man, but used the circumstance to make a quick introduction. Regardless of the method or methods you use, you and the people in your church have relationships all around that can become the conduit for sharing Christ.

Teach People

The flip side shows churches revising their discipleship programs every three to five years. Congregations invest in Sunday School, small groups, life groups, life tracks, new members classes, men's classes, women's classes, and other discipleship variations. Senior pastors champion ways to "close the back door" by keeping new Christ-followers by looking how to help them be an active part of the church. This discipleship attitude highlights teaching, and churches with this mindset often reduce the exodus through the back door by stopping the emphasis on getting them in the front one.

The arguments further divide the discipleship crowd over the content, location, and activities that constitute the perfect discipleship program. While discipleship programs seem to have a longer shelf life than evangelistic ones, how many people stop to ask the key questions of purpose with a long-range plan?

What if the school system where your child is enrolled approached long-term education the way your church does? Would it help or hurt your child if each teacher picked at random what he or she wanted to teach? Would your child be prepared for life if he or she could pick the subjects to study? What if the students selected only electives? In the same way, you must ask yourself and your team a foundational question: *If adults, teens, or children stay in our discipleship program for two, four, or six years, what will they learn, and how will it help them approach life?*

Why Choose?

So why do churches choose to emphasize either evangelism or discipleship? It typically comes down to the leaders' gifting and previous success. Football teams will either take on an offensive or defensive powerhouse based upon the coach's strengths unless the coach realizes the limitations and hires assistant coaches to fill that gap. Just as a football team cannot compete on a long-term basis with only a defensive or offensive mindset, a church cannot sustain growth and keep the same people who are part of the growth without both a reach and a teach approach.

When you hear a sermon or teaching on the Great Commission, the normal content is outreach and missions. We need to hear the "Go reach," but each of the Great Commission passages implies "Teach them" within the verse or context, so the cycle continues. Even Acts 1:8 carries over to Peter's great message in Acts 2. There, the people heard in their native language, but if you look further, you will find Peter challenging them to follow Christ so the next generation and the next will do the same. He did not stop with the call to repentance; the next verse describes how the church devoted themselves to the teaching of the apostles—discipleship.

The implication is obvious: go reach and teach so they can go reach. By the way, many often think the Great Commission requires a passport, but time around the dinner table is also a large part of our responsibility. Who is teaching dads and moms to have conversations that cultivate little ones to find Christ and grow in their knowledge of Scripture in the homes? When it comes to reach and teach, Christ's command is not an either/or, but a both/and. Throughout Scripture, you find that reach and teach go together in powerful ways and with God-honoring results.

A Reach and Teach Strategy

What should the reach and teach approach look like? Take a look at healthy churches instead of just the largest ones. If a church is experiencing spiritual and numerical growth in any increments, then several typical characteristics are present. These include both outreach and discipleship, neither of which can occur at random. The three levels of the reach and teach strategy discussed here come from long-standing, proven principles combined with some defined characteristics from a leading pastor on developing an effective family-centric ministry in a growing church.[2] One of those characteristics is a place where smaller groups of people can meet for a purpose. What then is the purpose, and what do these small groups look like?

I was in a church recently of just under a thousand members and heard one of the ministry leaders announce to guests that the church offers nearly 100 small groups. I wondered if there was a strategy beyond the individual purpose of each one. With such a large number of groups, how do they measure the success and health of each one?

Commanders on the battlefield know their mission and strategy (principles) before they decide what tactics or activities (programs) will be used to accomplish the mission. So many times pastors put tactics and activities ahead of strategy because they can see quick wins this way, but these programs are often unsustainable. Besides, church programs change faster than a man with the TV remote clicks away from Lifetime Movie Network™ when his wife leaves the room. You find and keep strategies, but you consistently revise tactics and programs.

Connection Groups: A Three-Level Strategy

The following strategy for a three-level connection group works for any size church. For the purposes of this book, the language will be more descriptive than promotional. You can choose names for each level that best represent your church later, but for now just grasp the distinctions. The reach and teach approach uses three levels to move people from non-Christ followers to solid disciples. To accomplish the movement, this approach, like any, relies on relationships and training. The people in your church need to be trained to facilitate and teach at the appropriate level. Level One is solely about outreach and building relationships. Level Two continues the outreach strategy by providing a community to help with felt needs. Level Three is the goal for all people, where deeper, consistent discipleship occurs.

Connection Group Level One

These groups never meet at church. They involve getting people from your congregation to lead interest groups at various times and locations. They tend to be activity-focused and might include something like a golf connection group where people meet in the early evening and play nine holes together once a week. Other connection groups could center around interests such as X-Box, board games, quilting, skateboarding, running, soccer, fishing, skeet shooting, and as many others as the interests in your church and community. This provides a chance to connect with people outside the church building. Make it your goal to have a mix in each group of no more than thirty percent church people leaving seventy plus percent who do not attend.

PATH OF REACHING & TEACHING

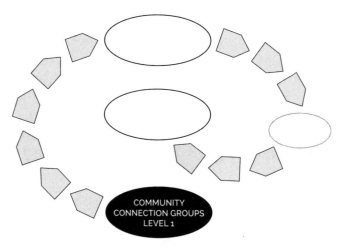

COMMUNITY
CONNECTION GROUPS
LEVEL 1

This non-threatening environment allows people in your church to get to know community neighbors (and vice versa) for longer periods as they talk, laugh, and play together. Real connections are made, and this provides a foundation on which to build. At the end or somewhere in the middle of the connection group meeting (whichever seems more natural), the leader should gather people and share a single encouraging verse of Scripture. At this stage, frame the discussion around relational tips, goals, or encouragement rather than preaching.

After reading and making brief comments about the verse, which should not take more than three or four minutes, take time to pray. With a small group of ten or fewer, you can ask for one request from each person before praying. Phrase it like this: "How can I pray for you this week?"

With this Level One group, you simply connect and let the Holy Spirit take down walls. Look for one-on-one time to go a bit deeper when you sense curiosity, and invite those individuals to your small group in your church. This approach gives every person in your church a chance to be a part of the thirty percent because everyone has a talent or hobby to just share. You mix up the group so people get to know each other based on projects or type of group.

Connection Group Level Two

Level Two groups might meet at church or somewhere else. They offer solutions to real life-felt needs. People look to the church to answer community problems, but often the church expects the community to be the solution for the church's needs. This is most unhealthy, dysfunctional, and somewhat codependent. Is it the mission of the church to reach people only so they can volunteer, give money, and fill seats in the sanctuary? People will quickly pick up on this selfish or inwardly focused attitude.

PATH OF REACHING & TEACHING

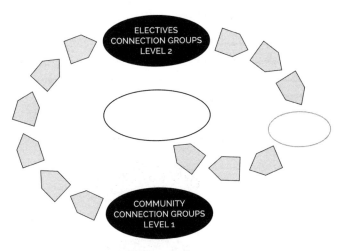

Level Two puts the church in a totally unselfish position to provide answers for life's problems such as grief, parenting, budgeting, retirement planning, addictions, healthy cooking, English as a second language (ESL), and others. The classes can also focus on electives like studying a specific book or Bible study. Curriculum is selected based on the topic and again, prayer is a part. As in Level One, you want to get people to realize that God cares about their lives, and their prayer requests help give them this awareness.

The goals of this level remain evangelistic and also include showing people a biblical basis for answers to life's problems. When someone is dealing with an addiction, for example, the church can show how freedom from this craving does not have to occur alone. This is a very different approach than those of secular programs. If the group deals with healthy cooking and meal preparation, it could offer a stewardship approach for balancing life according to the Bible—a key element also missing from secular programs.

In Level Two classes, you should work to maintain a membership of no more than fifty percent church people or less. If you get a lot of interest in a specific area or topic, divide the group to allow a safe, non-threatening environment for non-church people. The key is the facilitator's sensitivity in leading the group.

Connection Group Level Three

You eventually want to get everyone who attends church into a Level Three connection group. Levels One and Two focus on relationship-building and moving the group members into an openness to the idea of a deeper study among a community of Christ-followers. Level Three groups can meet at church or in homes—or both.

PATH OF REACHING & TEACHING

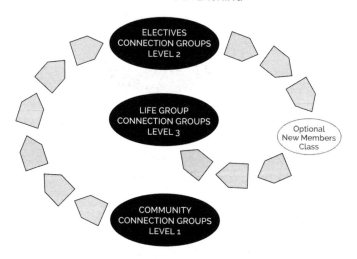

ELECTIVES
CONNECTION GROUPS
LEVEL 2

LIFE GROUP
CONNECTION GROUPS
LEVEL 3

Optional
New Members
Class

COMMUNITY
CONNECTION GROUPS
LEVEL 1

Churches call these life groups, connection groups, Sunday School, and other designations. But do not get hung up on names or assume this deeper level is no longer viable. Deeper-level study and intentional discipleship strategies are an integral part of growing, healthy churches. Connection groups for kids or youth offer a chance to provide a lesson and tools for parents to continue what the teacher started at church by coaching at home. The power of aligning families can be seen in Chapter 2, "1/168: Flawed Fraction or Ministry Multiplier?," but Level Three is where it happens.

Level Three also provides a curriculum for the teacher to work through. It should not be lecture-oriented, because interaction with students shows they are grasping and owning the material. Leaders of Level Three connection groups will want to include the following elements: prayer, teaching, connecting, and ways to look for how people can use their spiritual gifts. Teachers should look for potential teachers within their connection groups and mentor them, let them substitute, and help launch them into connection groups of their own. At this level, it is important to use a curriculum that teaches a balanced, comprehensive approach to Scripture over several years so new teachers and classes can benefit. Notice the final Level Three Connection Group has an on-ramp of a new member's class. Try to steer all new attendees and potential members through this short set of sessions. It will help them grasp their faith. Then identify their spiritual gifts and show them where they can use them. At the end of this set of sessions, help them land on a Level Three Connection Group.

	Level One	Level Two	Level Three
Goal	Evangelistic	Evangelistic	Discipleship
Location	Not Church	Church / Other	Church / home
Church People	>30%	>50%	Varies
Duration	8-16 weeks	4-12 weeks	13 weeks plus
Curriculum	No	Yes	Yes
Content Goal	Relationships	Felt Needs	Biblical Values
Content	Activity	Elective	Bible
Prayer	Yes	Yes	Yes
Connecting	Individuals	Communities	Families
Group Category	Community Connection	Elective Needs	Life Group

Ask yourself and your leadership the question, "If you give me your adults, teens, and children over six years, what will they know and who will they be at the end of this time?" Teach intentionally, and do so with a balanced approach of both Old and New Testaments. The Level Three material should be biblically-centered, and while it must deal with relevant life issues, it cannot be solely topical. In Level Three, parents and kids are taught the same family theme so parents can discuss the lessons with their kids without feeling unqualified or shrinking away from those conversations. This is where the church empowers parents while teaching all ages.

Reach and Teach: Both/And

It should be clear by now that you cannot choose to do just one. You cannot choose whether your church will reach or teach. You need both. Three levels with three distinct purposes but one strategy. Reach and teach. You are not asking all your members to be in all levels simultaneously. You want all members in Level Three, and want some of them leading Level One and Two or attending if life needs arise. The relationships of the people in your church will always provide the best opportunities to reach. By providing Level One and Level Two connection groups, you have a purposeful way to help people connect with your church and move toward deeper levels of discipleship that will stick for generations. And Scripture calls you to be both a reaching and a teaching church.

Methods for evangelism have certainly changed over time, but each requires relationships. The small group, Sunday School, life group, and connection groups have been proven models, but often receive the blame when a church begins to decline. If these groups decline, your church will decline, and vice-versa.

Instead of leading your church to change to the latest evangelistic method, change the way these groups work to reach and teach. What else can reach, connect, teach, mentor, and align families, all with the same effort? Done right, connection groups will bring the two types of growth every church needs: outward (numerical) and inward (spiritual).

D6 Connection

Questions

- Does your church have a strategy for reaching and teaching or does it work hard on programs and activities?
- Do your staff or volunteer leaders have greater gifting in evangelism or discipleship (make a list and see if you lack balance)?
- What intentional ways do people of your church connect with non-Christ followers and those who may not even have church on their radar?
- Analyze your curriculum for small groups and see if it fits Level One, Two, or Three strategies—see chart on page 89.
- Create a list of hobbies/passions and interests of members then mentor them (2 or 3 at a time to start Level One groups) and over a year see what happens, but have the end goal of Level Three ready.

Resources

Level One resources: your list of member's hobbies and talents

Level Two resources:

- Financial Peace University
- Grief Studies
- Celebrate Recovery
- Radical
- Divorce Care
- Visionary Parenting
- Visionary Marriage
- Any felt need study

Level Three resources:

- D6 2nd Generation Curriculum
- D6 Devotional Study Guides
- D6 Family App

10 Helping Parents Dive Deep

Connect to your kids, so you can help connect them
to God.[1] —Dannah Gresh

"Mountains or ocean?" That's a great question to ask when getting to know someone better. Which do they prefer for a vacation spot?

If you ask my wife, she will quickly respond, "The ocean!" while grabbing her umbrella and beach chair. She grew up in Ohio, while I hail from Florida. You might guess that my contrary answer leaves me grabbing my hiking boots and flannel shirt as I decide which peak to conquer—or think about conquering while sitting by the campfire. So yes, when deciding where to spend our vacation, I put my flip-flop-wearing foot down as I haul the overstuffed beach bag to the car.

One day, while enjoying the palm trees with all the vigor of scaling a summit, I noticed a principle that would help parents communicate better. It includes three simple, memorable visuals to help describe ways parents connect with their kids: sand castles, snorkels, and scuba.

Think of these three activities as the various depths of conversations and the way parents rarely wade out to the deeper depths, opting instead to stay on *terra firma*. While playing in the sand is fun, surface-level conversations never allow families to experience the depths of the ocean with its world of possibilities. By the end of this chapter, you will be able to use these three visuals to help coach parents in utilizing all three types of conversations to draw closer to the heart of their child or teenager.

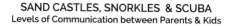

SAND CASTLES, SNORKLES & SCUBA
Levels of Communication between Parents & Kids

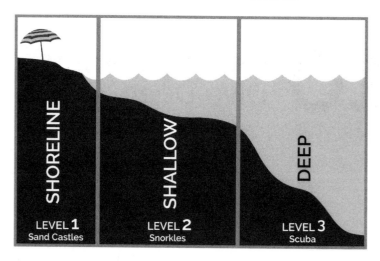

Level One—Sand Castles

The three levels of communication as depicted in the graph also correspond to the people who occupy that space. Few of them go deep. When you visit the ocean, the area where people build sand castles is more crowded than any other. And just as people are not always comfortable wading out into the water, parents are not always comfortable getting past the surface level of communication as depicted by Level One.

It is fun to watch parents interact with their kids, especially in public environments. In years past, my wife and I would play a restaurant game with our pre-teenaged kids. It entailed watching and talking together about that family (there's always one) in the restaurant with misbehaving kids. Sure, it sounds unkind, but oh, what teachable moments it gave us.

I know what you are thinking—was it not awkward to have four sets of eyes watching from a nearby table? Come on! Those parents were either oblivious or consumed by trying to fix the behaviors of their kids (controlling behavior rather than teaching values is the first of many parenting mistakes). And watching parents on the beach can be amusing for the exact same reasons—they are either scared their kids are going to drown or hoping they might.

On the sand, you find beach chairs, towels, umbrellas, and yes, sand castles. The sand castle space is Level One of communication, or surface-level. It includes the classic high-low questions: "What was the high point of your day?" "What was the low point of your day?"

The key to getting kids talking comes from two approaches. One is to ask open-ended (not yes or no) questions and to actually listen when they talk. Another comes from a game we used to play with our kids. In this "toss the ball" approach, we had an imaginary ball. When someone tossed a ball by asking you a question, you answered it and tossed the ball by asking one back. Tossing and responding to question after question helps kids learn to interact, be good conversationalists, and learn not to drop the ball in discussions.

Level One is about swapping knowledge updates from child to parent and hopefully vice versa. These swaps carry little risk, but also little investment because they concern surface-level events. The answers to such questions will rarely create any conflict and, as such, are safe. This interaction is safe because it is the level and type your kids might have with anyone.

However, when conversations are safe, parents and kids miss connecting at a deeper level. Remind the dads and moms in your church that they would never have married their spouse if they had only communicated at a surface level. If you can't win your spouse's heart with this sand level communication, why do you default to it with your kids?

Only when parents go deeper do they uncover emotional connections and a deeper level of thinking. But dealing with deeper levels may uncover uncomfortable topics, opposing values, and a potential inability to answer questions. Avoiding Levels Two and Three is understandable, but not best.

Level 1 Communication: Sand Castles—
Conversations about Knowledge

- Most parents are here—in the sand
- Asking simple experience questions
- Swapping knowledge about the day
- Little or no risk in the conversation

Our kids are now in college, but when they were just going off to kindergarten and first grade, my wife packed them yummy lunches every day. And every day, I would use a marker to draw a picture and write a note on their paper napkins telling them I loved them or was proud of them. While the pictures were only basic line drawings of butterflies, trees, hearts, and flowers, I later found out that their friends loved them and asked to see them each day.

As our kids grew, the napkin notes faded away. Instead, I would write two or three sentences of encouragement each day, along with a Bible verse, and print them from my computer. No pictures, no color, just a parent connecting at a heart level with his kids' lives.

This story from fifteen-plus years ago has inspired other parents toward similar activities. However, you need to recognize this as another example of Level One communication—one-way talk that builds knowledge into kids. While it may address their feelings and has definite value, it does not involve listening or discussing anything.

While Level One is easiest at the early childhood level, the older your child gets, the deeper your conversations should grow. And you will need to teach the parents in your church to go deeper. Some get stuck in the mode of thinking the way they dealt with their kids as young children will work all through their teen years. But God is developing parents and their kids at the same time. As parents of little ones, the majority of the conversations they have will be Level One. But as the kids grow into upper elementary, parents' conversations should grow along with them into Levels Two and Three.

Level 2—Snorkels

Our family has enjoyed taking cruises for some of our vacations. On a couple of them, my kids and I went snorkeling. While I enjoyed myself, I spent most of my time looking around and above the surface to ensure they were not choking. It is so easy to let the top of the snorkel dip too low and let in just a little water.

Snorkeling has become a favorite of ours because it opens up a world that you just cannot see from the surface of the ocean. Just as pictures never quite capture the beauty of the Grand Canyon, there is no substitute for seeing the fish up close or taking in the coral reefs and colors of the ocean. As the saying goes, you just have be there to understand it.

In the same way that snorkeling allows a slightly deeper ocean experience, a snorkel level of communication goes a bit deeper and includes asking about kids' feelings and opinions. The questions move from Level One, in which parents ask about the high and low points of their child's day, to Level Two, exploring more of the answers. If the Level One low point occurred when the coach removed a parent's son or daughter from the game, a Level Two question asks, "How did that make you feel?"

Remind the parents in your church that they must help their kids process their feelings in light of the best way to respond. When negative emotions come into play, parents should help navigate with ethics and values. But it is equally important that they teach their kids the right way to think, feel, and conduct themselves in positively charged emotional situations. And no parent knows what a child is thinking without asking. This gives them the chance to coach the kids' thinking process and help them evaluate the issues and emotions. The goal of Level Two is to help the child understand and process his feelings in light of Scripture, ethics, and community norms (in that order of importance).

Because these discussions involve asking about emotions and opinions, parents should not expect instant agreement. Remind them that the goal is not to force compliance, but to walk themselves and their kids through the principles of an evaluation process. This level of communication is very much a two-way exchange in which parents listen as much as they talk.

Yes, conflicts and disagreements will occur, making Level Two more challenging than Level One, but encourage the parents in your church not to avoid them. Don't retreat back to the sand of Level One. If Dad and Mom don't help their kids work through these essential issues, someone else will. Guide them to realize they are the best ones to influence their kids, especially when they can do so from a scriptural perspective.

Level 2 Communication: Snorkels— Conversations about Understanding

- Many parents are here—shallow but in the water
- Asking about feelings and opinions
- Looking for ways to coach their kids' mental processing
- Some risk in the conversation

Level 3—Scuba

Strapping on an oxygen tank means two obvious things: you are going deep and you will need help breathing. This also describes Level Three communication, in which the risk becomes greater and the conflict can get stronger. Level One dealt with knowledge, facts, and events of one's day. Level Two dug into opinions and feelings. In Level Three, parents and kids dive still deeper into desires, needs, and beliefs. All three levels work well when coached from scriptural values by a parent.

At this stage, real influence occurs. When parents stay at Levels One and Two, they must realize their child's friends go with them to Level Three, and often led by emotions and desires versus wisdom and values. When people discuss feelings and opinions, they need objectivity. Level Three helps shape our feelings, thinking, and reactions. The human reaction to someone hurting us is to lash back, but Level Three allows parents to springboard from the natural human emotional response to the biblical admonition. The paradigm shift occurs when kids grow enough to realize the response God expects is less about them and more about helping another, as clearly worded by Paul in Romans 12 (a Level Three conversation).

Maslow's hierarchy of needs, pictured in the next graphic, shows how the foundational areas must be addressed before moving toward the more complex areas. The pinnacle should be self-actualization, in which a person determines how they respond to morality, removes prejudice, and objectively works through issues. It is easy to see that when someone struggles with sexual issues (the love and belonging tier), he or she may also struggle with everything above that tier, such as self-esteem and morality, and skew the facts of right and wrong.

In this hierarchy, nearly every tier builds on the next. If a drowning man fears the lack of oxygen (the first or physiological tier), he may unknowingly drown his rescuer by reaching for safety (the second tier). Both teens and adults need to feel close to someone, thus the desire for friendships, family, and sexual intimacy. But when teens find the sense of belonging to a group, gang, or set of friends outside of the value system of parents, their confidence hangs on the new group's affirmation, and they interpret a new set of facts reflecting this group's worldviews. You can see how one violates other tiers to find ones most needed and this occurs in absence of biblical worldview.

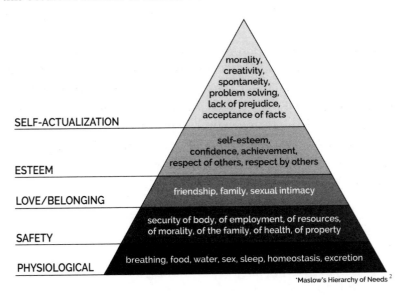

*Maslow's Hierarchy of Needs [2]

Before you think too harshly of teens making such choices, realize why ministers fall into sexual sin. Maslow identified the innate desire for sex (lowest and most basic need—differing from sexual intimacy). This explains why ministers have sometimes thrown away everything above that bottom tier to obtain sexual satisfaction—including safety, employment, family, respect, and certainly morality.

Before you think I have gone all psychological, let's examine some biblical parallels to Maslow. Paul warned that some must marry for sexual intimacy, needing this in order to avoid other sins (1 Cor. 7). Proverbs champions the value and wisdom of parents and the sense of belonging and building up a child (Proverbs 1:8-9, 3:11-12, 3:21-23, 4:23, and many more, pretty much all of Proverbs). Both Proverbs and Ecclesiastes warn that sexual sin outside of marriage can mar and damage intimacy, esteem, and respect (Proverbs 5 and 7, Ecclesiastes 2:1-13). And the Bible is quite clear that any prejudice against other races is an affront to our Creator as it disrespects others and lowers self-esteem when people feel threatened, violating their sense of security and safety (Rom. 10:12, 2:11, James 2:1-9, John 13:34-35, Prov. 22:2, Rev. 7:9, Luke 10:29-37). The reason more Christians cannot defend their faith is that they are stuck somewhere below the top tier of Maslow and the stage where the Bible says they are still infants when they should be eating meat and being students of the Word.

Where are the parents in your church on this law scale? John Maxwell's "law of the lid" for leaders also applies here. Apply this to parenting and it suggests that children will not typically rise to a level above the morality, beliefs, and views of their parents.[3] Then apply it to communication, and Level Three engages the kids on a deeper level in discussions about such areas. The place where the parent and kid overlap in such engaging conversation is the place where parents will find the potential for influence.

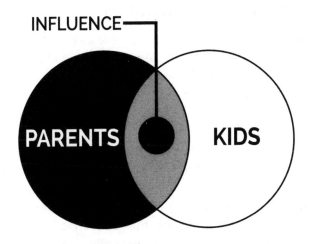

Level Three is messy, but just as the snorkel takes participants off-shore to see some amazing things, the scuba level takes them deeper still and brings them up close to worlds they never imagined. In the same way, Jesus knew how to get past the surface-level questions to more probing ones that would influence people's thinking. Read His narrative with Nicodemus, (John 3:1-21), the woman at the well (John 4:7-30), Peter beside the fire after Christ's resurrection (John 21:1-17), Judas after the fateful kiss on the cheek (Matt. 26:47-50; Luke 22:47-48) and Martha when complaining about Mary (Luke 10:38-42). While Christ is bound by no man's theory, we do see where Maslow's hierarchy applies, as Jesus would often meet a physical need before dealing with a spiritual one.

Level 3 Communication: Scuba—
Conversations of Influence

- Few parents are here—deep
- Asking about desires, needs, and beliefs
- Addressing the foundational needs for moral strength
- Greatest potential for shaping values
- High possibility of conflict and disagreement

Three Levels of Communication

Just as you would not encourage a diver to go from the beach to the depths of the sea without adequate preparation, do not encourage parents to jump right into Level Three. Dads and moms reacting to their teenager's bad decisions often make this mistake. And because they never went to this depth in regular conversations, the teenager resents the sudden intrusion.

The daily family routine should include working through levels One and Two, and as opportunity presents itself from life circumstances and conversations, engaging at Level Three. While I am not espousing a formula for the frequency of Level Three conversations, parents should make sure they happen more than once a week, and not only at church. This depth should not feel like unfamiliar territory. Daily working through Levels One and Two should cause parents to bump into Three regularly. Model and teach these three levels of communication for the parents in your church:

- Level One: Sand Castles—Conversations about Knowledge
- Level Two: Snorkels—Conversations about Understanding
- Level Three: Scuba—Conversations of Influence

Realize that Levels One and Two are a means for parents to understand and empathize with their kids in order to gain the opportunity to shape their beliefs, desires, and needs. It is amazing what kids describe as *needs* which, in reality, are wants. But parents can help them discern the difference. Parents can also help their kids see how justifying human desires is a result of ignoring the authority of Scripture. Level Three challenges how people think and, inadvertently, how they feel and behave.

Have you taught the parents of your church how to have conversations at all three levels? Their kids will never remember some of the conversations Dad and Mom have with them, but if they do not have them at all, rest assured: Their kids will never forget.

D6 Connection

Questions

Ask parents in the church:

- How similar are the deep-rooted values of your kids compared to the parents?
- How often do you get to talk about the highs and lows of each day?
- Do your kids understand how to "toss the ball" back and forth during conversation?
- When is the last time values and/or Scripture were shared during regular conversations?
- Have the parents list Level One, Level Two, and Level Three and then put check marks each time these conversations occur over the next 30 days.

Resources

52 Creative Family Time Experiences by Timothy Smith

Legacy Path by Brian Haynes

Visionary Parenting by Rob Rienow

Boundaries With Teens: When to Say Yes and How to Say No by John Townsend

It Starts at Home: A Practical Guide to Nurturing Lifelong Faith by Kurt Bruner and Steve Stroope

Faith Conversations for Your Families by Jim Burns

D6 Family App

D6 Devotional Study Guides

SPLINK

11 Changing the Way People Think

We change our behavior when the pain of staying the same becomes greater than the pain of changing. Consequences give us the pain that motivates us to change.[1]—Dr. Henry Cloud

Don't you wish it were possible to open a door on the back of people's heads and swap out either the entire brain—or at least the part that would cause their preferences to line up with yours? This would eliminate the need for persuasion, logic, inspiration, and yes, leadership. Have you heard a pastor say that the hardest part about pastoring is the congregation? The most difficult aspect of leadership is getting buy-in from the people you lead.

Looking back through history, when was the first known shift of thinking in any group? You are, no doubt, familiar with the story. Satan, in the form of an attractive being, cast a new vision for Eve in which she could be better and more capable. She voiced concerns. He countered, persuasively. She bought in—or should we say, "bit in"?

At that point, Satan's vision for change and Eve's persuasive tactics created a coalition to help convince Adam to eat the fruit (often referred to as an apple). Their culture changed, but not in the right direction, and certainly not in a way that benefited anyone except the one attempting to change others.

Leadership Defined

John Maxwell suggests that leadership can be defined in one word—influence.[2] That definition sounds so accurate but is in fact quite flawed.

As a child, I played the game Mercy, where you lock fingers and see who can bend the other's hands backward to the point where he cries, "*Mercy!*," which determines the winner. Many games have ended with this consenting cry, and at opportune times, you could ask the other person to agree to almost anything because they felt like every finger was about to break. You could ask them to say you were the smartest, they were ugly, and even get them to agree to perform certain tasks. In this situation, you might say you had influence over your victim, but few would consider this leadership.

This is a simplistic way of showing how dictators such as Stalin, Noriega, bin Laden, Hussein, and Hitler should never be called leaders. The influence they wielded came from fear tactics and coercion, not leadership. Like these dictators, Satan also coerces with his temptation tactics as he leaves behind morality and collective good.

Just as dictators cannot truly be considered leaders, a mere title does not make you a leader, either. When a military officer receives his or her commission, rank is given on that day, but for every day after, leadership will need to be earned. The fact remains—leadership involves relationships. And when a person leads, the existence of followers is implied.

So how does one define leadership? Northouse, one of today's premier leadership scholars, suggests that leadership happens "when one individual influences a group of individuals to achieve a common goal."[3]

You say, "That's it—that's what I am trying to do." But look at three words in this definition to determine if leadership is truly happening. The first, "influence" distinguishes from a dictatorial style—which rarely has positive, lasting effects—and a transformational style that invests in people and works toward collective, beneficial goals. Influence does not rely on titles, leverage, or power. Instead, it requires a leader who casts an inspiring vision and direction by showing the benefit of what achieving this goal will do for the common good or, in ministry terms, for the Kingdom.

The other two words, "common goal," represent the second area leaders often hurry past. Either you think up great ideas on the spot, or you crockpot them and let them simmer for a few days or weeks. But when you reveal a new idea or goal to the congregation, never forget that they are hearing it for the very first time. Don't expect them to microwave their acceptance when it took you several weeks of slow cooking it. You took time to process it, analyze, and refine it, and they deserve the same consideration.

When and how to present the idea is another major part of getting people to adopt it. If you do not present it in the right way, your people may reject it for the wrong reasons. But without personal affirmation and adoption of the idea, the people may comply, but only outwardly.

After all, dictators get outward obedience for a while because they selfishly push for the win and the credit, believing they are the only ones who are right. Leaders, however, operate differently, patiently helping their followers find the worth in the new idea. They also invite followers to help in shaping the idea and implementation. When people see and value the goals in the same way their leader does, they will exert enormous energy to help achieve those common goals.

Compliance or Collaboration?

Goals usually require changing the status quo. This change often necessitates a change in culture that compels people toward a different disposition. Why disposition? Remember, you are not looking for a simple behavioral change in followers, as that would imply mere compliance. When leaders only want obedience, their followers give little effort in sustained change. Prison wardens get conformity from the inmates, employers get work from employees, and parents can use intimidation, guilt, or force to demand obedience from their kids.

In all these situations, the end result is similar to what happened when Jonah preached to Nineveh. As the city caught revival, Jonah pouted. Why? He obeyed and preached but never really bought into the goal. He cared only about himself and forgot the common goal of thousands submitting to God. His attitude stunk!

So—God was the bad leader? No, but Jonah did require strong-arming as God "fished around" for a tactic that would work. Jonah went, but not because he wanted to. God had to work with him a little bit more in order for Jonah to see the big picture (Jonah 4).

Congregations often feel pressured to yield to the pastor. Leaders should help followers mentally work through the adoption of the goals so they willingly put forth the effort needed to attain the mutually desired outcome.

Leadership occurs when *one* engages people to influence their values without the use of force. This is accomplished by building and inspiring the followers' collaboration and growth toward the collective moral good of the culture. Now, take out the word *one,* insert your ministry title, and reread the definition—twice.

Soak in the fact that you are called to help shape how individual people, who make up the collective body of the church, can aspire to help the mission of the congregation. This often requires a shift in thinking. And when you change how people think, you change cultures.

Changing the Culture

Lasting change requires more than causing new behaviors. Let me confess through my own failure what this means. In my first pastorate, I redesigned the church logo, removed the outdated rails above the altar to open the look of the stage, took down the old-school number boards that showed attendance, and hid the small church bank that collected birthday pennies each Sunday. While the church experienced solid numerical and financial growth, when I left three years later, all the items I listed as changed were put back as if they had never changed.

In this situation, I failed to lead. Leadership includes followers and helps them see the need for change. When they adopt and work toward goals, it is only because they recognize its benefits. I failed as a leader because I changed the looks and not the culture of the church.

In order to change cultures, you need to become a student of change. Read about how historical leaders helped show people how to think so differently that their behavior, routines, policies, and customs changed to match. Some cultural change leaders worth studying include Martin

Luther, Gandhi, William Wilberforce, William Carey, Martin Luther King, Jr., and America's Founding Fathers. Note some characteristics of steps to church cultural change:

- Leaders help people (not just other leaders) recognize a need for change
- Leaders communicate the value and advantage of the change
- Leaders inspire the group toward moral right even if not immediately advantageous
- Leaders create a team of influential people from the group to establish a plan
- Leaders enable and empower the team to influence the group
- Leaders and team help the group to see and experience solutions
- Leaders celebrate changes and wins with the group
- Leaders are patient as cultural change occurs over time[4]

Principles of Change

The staff, the volunteers, and the congregation need someone to lead and model a direction for everyone to follow. The leader cannot simply point and say, "Go that way!" The leader must describe the destination, the path along the way, and why this particular objective is crucial. Leadership casts a collective goal by helping people see the benefits of changing paths. Chapter 7, "Staffing for a D6 Church," elaborates more on the topic of why leaders must be the adhesive for the team.

When you read about George Washington, John Adams, Alexander Hamilton, Thomas Jefferson, and Benjamin Franklin, you see that these Founding Fathers did not originally set out to create the United States of America. In fact, Washington's greatest goal in life up until the French and Indian War was to receive a commission in the British Army within one of the four districts in the colonial government for the king. The breakdown in relations between the colonists and Britain, however, revealed a different set of goals. The Founding Fathers began to suggest an experiment that would involve a government not ruled by a monarchy. They proposed a representative form of government with three branches: executive, legislative, and judicial, with the executive and legislative branches accountable to the people.

Such an outlandish concept was neither popular nor easy. It is very hard for patriotic Americans today to conceive of a time when the colonists wanted to belong to another nation, stay under its protection, and go without our own national identity. But at the time, most people would have called the idea of a "united states" absurd, as no other great nation used this form of government.

Benjamin Franklin, ever the innovator, suggested an experiment that would show how this different form of government could work. The Continental Congress appointed five of its members to serve on a committee to draft language that birthed the experiment. Roger Sherman, Robert Livingston, Ben Franklin, John Adams, and a very young Thomas Jefferson were appointed to represent five prominent states and write a draft. Congress debated for several days before voting on July 4, 1776 for the Declaration of Independence.

The Founding Fathers modeled the set of change principles noted earlier to shift the British mindset of the royal colonies to become American colonies and later form the experiment called the United States of America. The Declaration of Independence outlined the major vision statement and later, the Constitution provided some tactical framework for how the experiment could be accomplished.

Due to the Constitution's lack of popularity among the colonies (later called states) and especially in New York, *The Federalist Papers* were written to describe why the path chosen would be helpful for everyone involved. That particular set of writings by Alexander Hamilton, James Madison, and John Jay helped convince people to vote for the Constitution in 1788. But the great experiment took another twelve years to get almost everyone on board.

Significant change is a process, not an event. Reread the previous bulleted list as you review the change led by our Founding Fathers and note the significance of each step.

It all started with casting vision and providing the identity found in the Declaration of Independence. While it took years to gain adequate support and over a decade to ratify the U. S. Constitution, the change process worked. America is far from perfect, but it offers liberties unlike most other nations. People still cross oceans, traverse rivers, and travel great distances to be a part of the experiment that became a collective benefit to all citizens.

The changing of the colonists' British mindset did not occur on July 4, 1776, but through leaders who understood how to shape thinking and knew that one day, the patriotic behaviors would follow. Nearly ninety years later, Lincoln reminded divided Americans about the foundations of this experiment and vision cast by the Founding Fathers for their "new nation, conceived in liberty, and dedicated to the proposition that all men are created equal."[5] And one hundred years later, Martin Luther King, Jr. would use this same change process and the language of the Declaration of Independence to argue for another shift in culture that affirmed the truth that "all men are created equal," including African-Americans. And it all began with leaders who cast a vision for a set of ideals and patiently communicated, pursued, inspired, and championed their goals over time until the collective people found the same passion to do the same for the mutual benefit of all.

Beware Groupthink

The best-laid vision statement can be derailed by one influential comment stated early in the discussion, causing others to shy away from adoption as well. This phenomenon, called groupthink, occurs when you are sitting in a meeting and the group is considering a potential decision. One influencer in the group speaks in favor of or in opposition to a certain outcome and no one wants to counter that voice.

Groups tend to gravitate to consensus rather than conflict or arguments over opposing possibilities. In Christian circles, people give in far too often to groupthink and allow poor decisions to occur rather than risk hurting someone's feelings. Never confuse getting support with getting the vote.

A wise leader can overcome groupthink by spending time with key influencers before the meeting takes place. By going to certain individuals ahead of time, you are not lobbying for your outcome but helping them think through the problem and possible solutions prior to the group meeting. Remember, the goal is not to get your way, but to find the right way. Listening to people's thoughts and ideas helps; they often have better solutions than you do. Visiting four to six key influencers prior to an important meeting could alter the solution you present and most likely the outcome as well.

In order to move large groups of people passionately toward a collective goal, you must give each of the group members the opportunity to wrestle with the issues. People can and do follow even when not thoroughly convinced of the decided direction. But they will stay the course more readily if they have heard various possibilities, had a chance to weigh in, and considered the pros and cons of each possible outcome.

Groups do not want leaders dictating a direction for them to rubber-stamp. They do want decisive leaders who pause and listen. Implementing various ways to involve the counsel of more experts and have them represented at the decision-making process will yield a stronger outcome, as it did for the United States when Thomas Jefferson attended the meeting to draft the Declaration of Independence.

The Change Process

If you want change to last, don't rush it. You can change environments rather quickly, but you change cultures over time. I recently participated in a strategic change process for a large church. The leadership invited eight church members to participate. This group met about every three weeks for ninety minutes each time over a three- or four-month period. Some lessons gained from this typical change or planning group will help show others how to steer the church into a place to minister effectively based upon the right criteria.

First meetings can often look scattered, with people asking random questions or asserting various opinions. The pastor, if leading this meeting, cannot take a heavy-handed approach (destination already determined, too defensive, or playing any variation of the passive-aggressive card). Leading sometimes means allowing others to discover in order to buy in and own the direction. Most important to the process is that you are seeking the right direction, not your own direction.

This church was not dying but was not growing, either. The people in the room talked about its history and acknowledged key moments while asking some insightful and tough questions. At the end of the first meeting, a couple of people in the room may have felt frustrated since few or no answers were reached. In order for people to help plan the future, they must understand the past and assess the present. Only after that are they able to realize the potential.

The second meeting included two exercises that prompted progress. A SWOT (Strengths, Weaknesses, Opportunities, and Threats) analysis was conducted to highlight key building blocks and identify potential eroding factors in the health of the church. The exercise took only thirty minutes as the group was timed for each category of answers, listing them on a whiteboard.

At the end of the exercise, the group looked for converging thoughts across all four categories and quickly spotted three or four. These would serve as the church's DNA. Next, the pastor challenged the group to look for ways to make the church healthier. "In real life, a person has a core DNA and may be prone to certain physical conditions," he told us. "But that person can work out, take supplements, eat right, and improve the condition and their overall health. And the same thing is true for a church."

During the second meeting, the group suggested some ideas for a rally cry, overarching theme, or secret sauce that the church could emphasize for every ministry. This particular church has a strong children's ministry and a solid seniors' group. One of its outreach ministries includes working with elementary schools in the community by offering Good News Clubs. Discussions ensued around a potential overarching theme like "developing spiritual gladiators" would mean that the Good News Clubs are not the sole responsibility of the children's ministry. Each of those children has parents, and the adult ministry should figure out what its role is in reaching them. Likewise, the senior adult ministry should always include the children's, as most seniors have grandchildren they care about. This type of cross-pollination occurs when leaders challenge the group with an overarching theme that is simple, memorable, and transferrable to every ministry of the church.

But the second meeting also produced some disagreements. When you bring people together to form or shape direction, do not be surprised if those with strong opinions suggest different ideas. And just because someone disagrees with you does not make him or her any less intelligent or concerned of the outcome. The second exercise of the meeting took the item of contention and randomly divided the group in half to argue both sides. Even if the group members were in favor of the idea, they were asked to present arguments against it. After switching sides and allowing time for each to frame the pro and cons, the right answer became apparent to everyone in the room. The contrast between first and second meetings was striking, but that is the process, and it takes time.

Choosing an overarching theme allows the church to measure progress, provide accountability, and decide what new areas to adopt or dismiss. This strategy dismantles the harmful, isolating silos and helps each member and ministry contribute and understand how to be part of the goal. In fact, every person should be asked, "What is your role in 'developing generational gladiators'?" or whatever your theme turns out to be.

Later meetings included settling on the exact wording of the theme and developing a measurable matrix containing goals for every ministry of the church that laid out what part they were to play in carrying out the overarching goal.

Another topic included was how to roll out the new ideas for the entire congregation, encouraging them to adopt the initiative rather than feel it was forced upon them. This last part, done poorly, could derail the entire process. You will need to move groups slowly through the same change progression and, if possible, have key influencers involved in the entire process, from the first meetings onward.

Think Different!

At the end of the day, leadership cannot be sustained by democracies led only by consensus. The opposite and unsustainable type is the group under control of a dictator who leads by authority or power. Leaders, by nature, often see further down the road than followers due to skill sets and experience, but ignoring followers' input and counsel is not wise. People may grant leaders occasional latitude for isolated decision-making, however, it is not the norm.

Reflect on how the change process is like a recipe: gather the ingredients, follow the steps, and never underestimate the amount of prep time you will need. The leader's job is to help the church see the consequences of actions either by showing them other churches that have followed the same path or alternatives with a new direction that changes the outcome. Either way, the leader is not simply *telling* the church what to do, but helping the church *discover* what to do. Leaders should spend the time needed to get people to believe in and work toward a collaborative direction. This is how cultures are changed and sustained.

I opened this chapter with the story of one who offered an "apple" for the wrong reason. But entrepreneur Steve Jobs offered people an Apple™ to change the culture. This brilliant executive intuitively led the company and gave some of his most inspirational sales pitches wearing his signature black pants, black mock turtleneck, and eccentric circle-rimmed glasses. He walked people through the simplicity of how to do the unimaginable and, in the process, inspired them to try what had never been done before. Apple™ brought us the mouse, the smart phone, digital music, apps, and no-wallet retail checkouts. And the vast cultural change the company accomplished all began by asking people to "Think Different!"

D6 Connection

Questions

- When you introduce change, how many other leaders do you involve prior to the whole congregation hearing about it?
- How long do you allow other leaders to help shape and adopt significant changes?
- Look at the bullet point list of church culture change steps (page 109) and rate yourself on a scale of 1-10 on how well you used these steps on your last change.

Resources
Leading Change (seminal work on change) by John Kotter

Diffusion of Innovation (the best work on change in my opinion) by Everett Rogers

Ministry Titles:

There's Hope for Your Church: First Steps to Restore Health and Growth by Gary Mcintosh

The Conviction to Lead by Al Mohler

Advanced Strategic Planning by Aubrey Malphurs

ReVision The Key to Transforming Your Church by Aubrey Malphurs

Spiritual Leadership by J. Oswald Sanders

Epilogue of Encouragement

Faith at home practices led by spiritually lethargic parents lead to spiritually lethargic children.[1]
—Richard Ross

Every ministry leader desires to make a bigger difference. Most leaders think in terms of organizational impact, but God thinks in terms of personal influence and more specifically, family impact. God included the numerous genealogies for a reason—how parents affect the thinking and future of generations is undeniable. The testimony moves from Genesis to Deuteronomy and on to Nehemiah who said, "Remember the Lord, who is great and awesome, and fight for your brothers, your sons, your daughters, your wives, and your homes" (Neh. 4:14b).

You can fail as a pastor, fail as a leader, but there is no greater fight than for your home. Paul continues that theme in Ephesians when he prayed that every family would find strength from the inside out to grow stronger in Christ. Furthermore, in that same prayer, Paul closes with the familiar wording, "Now to him who is able to do far more abundantly than all that we ask or think, according to the power at work within us, to him be glory in the church and in Christ Jesus *throughout all generations,* forever and ever. Amen" (Eph. 3:20-21).

Your church can change the culture of your community, our country, and even the world. Generational discipleship has no geographical boundaries, no limit to eras, and has always been the center of our Father's heart. Will you and your church help dads and moms honor and serve Him throughout all generations? Begin now to establish a new DNA in your church—D6, Generational Discipleship.

If you did not take your team through the free *DNA of D6 Generational Discipleship Assessment,* consider doing it now to help you and your leaders determine where you are right now. After self-scoring your results, you will have identified areas for improvement that correspond to various chapters found in this book. Consider having all of your small group leaders, staff, and lead volunteers take it with you. You can find it at d6family.com/dna.

Notes

Chapter 1—Where to Begin?

[1] Haynes, Brian, *The Legacy Path: Discover Intentional Spiritual Parenting* (Randall House, 2011), p. 4.

Chapter 2—1/168: Flawed Fraction or Ministry Multiplier?

[1] Hoffmaster, Thomas, sermon heard by Ron Hunter.

[2] https://www.barna.org/barna-update/culture/664-the-state-of-the-bible-6-trends-for-2014#.VO_rr7PF8wx.

[3] http://entertainment.time.com/2013/11/20/fyi-parents-your-kids-watch-a-full-time-jobs-worth-of-tv-each-week/.

[4] http://www.csun.edu/science/health/docs/tv&health.html#influence.

[5] Ibid.

[6] Ibid.

[7] https://www.barna.org/barna-update/culture/657-three-digital-life-trends-for-2014#.VctfzxNViko.

Chapter 3—D6 Goes Beyond Deuteronomy 6

[1] Haynes, Brian, *The Legacy Path: Discover Intentional Spiritual Parenting* (Randall House, 2011).

[2] VanderKam, James. C., *Dead Sea Scrolls Today* (Eerdmans, 1994).

[3] Christensen, Duane L., *Word Biblical Commentary Vol. 6a, Deuteronomy 1-21:9 (revised and expanded)* (Thomas Nelson, 2001).

[4] Woods, Edward J., *An Introduction and Commentary: Deuteronomy,* (Inter-Varsity Press, 2011).

[5] Kimmel, Tim, *Connecting Church and Home* (Randall House, 2013), p. 39.

[6] Lincoln, A. T., *Ephesians* (Word Books, 1990).

[7] Wilkinson, Bruce, *Experiencing Spiritual Breakthroughs: The Powerful Principle of the Three Chairs* (Multnomah, 1999).

[8] Ibid.

[9] Wright, Christopher, *Deuteronomy* (Hendrickson, 1996).

[10] Towns, Elmer, Presentation at East Coast Mid-Atlantic Christian Educators Association, 2004.

[11] Merrill, Eugene H., *The New American Commentary: Deuteronomy* (Broadman and Holman, 1994).

Chapter 4—Biblical Worldview and Battleships

[1] Ron Hunter.

[2] I need to acknowledge to any sailors reading this chapter that I realize the battleship is no longer part of the Navy's fleet. World War II proved the battleship obsolete and replaced it with the destroyer, which operates both offensively and defensively. But in most people's minds, the battleship and aircraft carrier are two of the most prominent surface vessels, and no one has named a game after the destroyer. Parents can apply everything this chapter suggests about battleships to building their kids into cruisers, destroyers, and other vessels of adaptable and capable abilities.

[3] Sire, James. W., *Naming the Elephant: Worldview as a Concept* (InterVarsity Press, 2004), p. 24.

[4] Sire, p. 27.

[5] Guba, Egon G., *The Paradigm Dialog* (Sage, 1990), p. 17.

[6] Naugle, David, *Worldview: The History of a Concept* (Eerdmans, 2002), p. 61.

[7] Bloom, Benjamin, *Taxonomy of Educational Objectives: The Classification of Educational Goals. New York* (David McKay, 1956).

Chapter 5—The One-Eared Mickey Mouse

[1] Jones, Timothy Paul, http://www.timothypauljones.com/2013/10/28/family-ministry-the-family-as-the-original-small-group-ministry/.

[2] Smith, Adam, Charles Bullock Editor, *Wealth of Nations* (Oxford World Classics, 1998) p. 12-13.

[3] http://www.pbs.org/wgbh/aso/databank/entries/dt13as.html.

[4] Cummings-Bond, Stuart, "The One-Eared Mickey Mouse," *Youthworker*, Fall 1989, p. 76.

Chapter 6—The Senior Pastor Complex

[1] Fix, Leneita, http://www.lifetreefamily.com/blog/become-spectators/.

[2] https://www.barna.org/index.php?option=com_content&view=article&id=644:prodigal-pastor-kids-fact-or-fiction&catid=15:familykids&Itemid=308#.VZrhR-1VhHw.

[3] Lewis, C.S., *The Screwtape Letters* (Harper Collins, 1996).

[4] https://www.barna.org/index.php?option=com_content&view=article&id=644:prodigal-pastor-kids-fact-or-fiction&catid=15:familykids&Itemid=308#.VZrhR-1VhHw.

[5] "Failure" And The Michael Jordan Underdog Myth; Nike Commercial, 1997.

[6] Rainey, Dennis, 2012 D6 Conference.

Chapter 7—Staffing for a D6 Church

[1] Lombardi, Vince, *What It Takes to be Number #1: Vince Lombardi on Leadership* (McGraw Hill Professional, 2001), p. 21.

[2] Carroll, Pete, http://mweb.cbssports.com/nfl/writer/jason-la-canfora/25016794/super-bowl-49-pete-carrolls-decision-astonishing-explanation-perplexing.

[3] Mike Trimble–Lead Pastor at Kirby Church has Volunteer Sunday every year.

[4] http://espn.go.com/college-football/story/_/id/9639274/florida-state-seminoles-shift-touted-safety-karlos-williams-rb.

http://espn.go.com/blog/acc/post/_/id/60033/karlos-williams-move-a-worthy-experiment.

http://www.cbssports.com/nfl/draft/players/1860763/karlos-williams.

http://www.cbssports.com/collegefootball/eye-on-college-football/24400958/video-florida-state-keeps-bcs-title-hopes-alive-with-fake-punt-vs-auburn.

http://www.buffalobills.com/news/article-1/On-Mother%E2%80%99s-Day-RB-Karlos-Williams-a-thankful-young-man/94a7fd1b-78f8-457e-bb38-0fffa95df0bc.

http://www.seminoles.com/ViewArticle.dbml?ATCLID=209572989.

[5] Richard Ross, *The Senior Pastor and the Reformation of Youth Ministry* (Lifeway/Church Resources, 2015), p. X.

[6] http://www.si.com/vault/2015/02/26/106731359/lessons-from-the-dean.

[7] Clark, Chap, *Youth Ministry in the 21st Century: Five Views* (Baker Academic, 2015).

Chapter 8—The Unseen Staff Member

[1] Luce, Sam, From podcast interview by Jeremy Lee on June 30, 2014 on Parenting Ministry Network discussing William Farley's book *Gospel-Powered Parenting: How the Gospel Shapes and Transforms Parenting* http://parentministry.net/podcast/episode-017-what-the-gospel-demands-of-parents-with-sam-luce/.

[2] Movie trailer, *Moneyball*, http://goo.gl/v4XkNi.

Chapter 9—Reach and Teach Strategy

[1] Kinnaman, Dave, *You Lost Me: Why Young Christians Are Leaving Church . . . and Rethinking Faith* (Baker Books, 2011), p. 13.

[2] The three level of connection groups presented in the DNA of D6 are a modified version presented by Tim York as a DMin. student at Liberty University.

His concept showed three groups in concentric circles and very similar principles.

Chapter 10—Helping Parents Dive Deep

[1] Gresh, Dannah, http://d6family.com/2014/09/four-reasons-parents-must-connect-to-their-child/.

[2] Maslow, A. H., *Motivation and Personality* (1st ed.) (Harper 1954).

[3] Maxwell, John, *The 21 Irrefutable Laws of Leadership: Follow Them and People Will Follow You* (Thomas Nelson, 2007), chapter 1.

Chapter 11—Changing the Way People Think

[1] Cloud, Henry and Townsend, John, *Boundaries with Kids: How Healthy Choices Grow Healthy Children* (Zondervan, 1998), p. 72.

[2] Maxwell, John, *Leadership 101—Inspirational Quotes and Insights for Leaders* (Thomas Nelson, 2002), p. 4.

[3] Northouse, Peter G., *Leadership: Theory and Practice* (Sage Publications, 2013), p. 5.

[4] List inspired by Kotter, John, *Leading Change* (Harvard Business Review Press, 2012), p. 21 and Rogers, Everett, *Diffusion of Innovations* (Free Press, 2003), p. 15-16

[5] Lincoln, Abraham, "The Gettysburg Address." Our Gettysburg Correspondence: The last of the dead buried, condition of the wounded, and the battlefield relic gatherers. (1863, July 15,). *The New York Times.*

Epilogue of Encouragement

[1] Richard Ross. D6 Conference, 2012.

NOTES

NOTES

NOTES

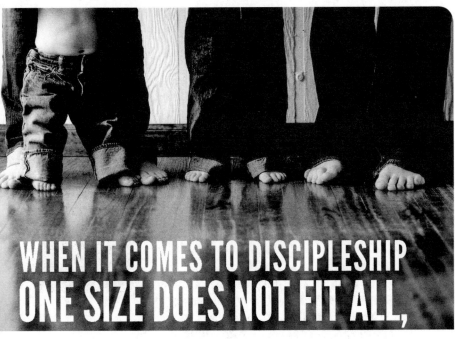

MORE FAMILY RESOURCES
from Randall House

**52 Creative Family
Time Experiences**

TIMOTHY
SMITH

**Connecting Church
and Home**

DR. TIM
KIMMEL

The Legacy Path

BRIAN
HAYNES

**Tech Savvy
Parenting**

BRIAN
HOUSMAN

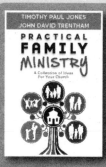

**Practical Family
Ministry**

TIMOTHY
PAUL JONES AND
JOHN DAVID
TRENTHAM

**Five Reasons for
Spiritual Apathy
in Teens**

ROB AND
AMY RIENOW